Novels in Verse for Teens

Verse novels offer the weight of each word, the weight of the sentence, the weight of the line, the weight of white space, heightened attention to sound, and deep allegiance to silence.

—*Rita Dove*

Novels in Verse for Teens

A Guidebook with Activities for Teachers and Librarians

Lisa Krok

LIBRARIES
UNLIMITED®

An Imprint of ABC-CLIO, LLC

Santa Barbara, California • Denver, Colorado

Library of Congress Cataloging-in-Publication Data

Names: Krok, Lisa, author.
Title: Novels in verse for teens : a guidebook with activities for teachers and
    librarians / Lisa Krok.
Description: Santa Barbara, California : Libraries Unlimited, [2020] | Includes
    bibliographical references and indexes.
Identifiers: LCCN 2019051210 (print) | LCCN 2019051211 (ebook) | ISBN
    9781440874932 (paperback) | ISBN 9781440874949 (ebook)
Subjects: LCSH: Teenagers—Books and reading—United States. | Novels in verse—
    Bibliography. | Novels in verse—History and criticism. | Readers' advisory services—
    United States. | Young adults' libraries—Activity programs—United States. | School
    libraries—Activity programs—United States. | Young adult literature—Study and
    teaching (Middle school)—United States. | Young adult literature—Study and
    teaching (Secondary)—United States. | Libraries—Special collections—Young
    adult literature. | Young adult fiction in libraries—United States
Classification: LCC Z1037.A1 K76 2020 (print) | LCC Z1037.A1 (ebook) |
    DDC 808.83/99283071—dc23
LC record available at https://lccn.loc.gov/2019051210
LC ebook record available at https://lccn.loc.gov/2019051211

ISBN: 978-1-4408-7493-2 (paperback)
        978-1-4408-7494-9 (ebook)

24 23 22 21 20   1 2 3 4 5

This book is also available as an eBook.

Libraries Unlimited
An Imprint of ABC-CLIO, LLC

ABC-CLIO, LLC
147 Castilian Drive
Santa Barbara, California 93117
www.abc-clio.com

This book is printed on acid-free paper. ∞

Manufactured in the United States of America

For marginalized teens and reluctant readers everywhere—
I see you.

Contents

PART ONE

Understanding and Using Novels in Verse

Getting Started: Why Use Novels in Verse?

Novels in Verse for Teens: A Guidebook with Activities for Teachers and Librarians includes not only details of verse novels that are available for use with teens, but also research-based information on how, why, and when to use them. A variety of book lists can be found online, but they give teachers and librarians only one piece of the puzzle. Readers' advisories are provided to assist with pairing books with teens based upon their grade level, needs, interests, and specific situations.

After teens are paired with books, activities are provided to engage them further with the poetry. This in turn empowers them to compose individual creative writing pieces using multiple styles of verse, such as narrative, acrostic, concrete, free verse, found poetry, contrapuntal, haiku, cinquain, memoirs, spoken word poetry, and more.

White Space

Verse novels are continuing to grow in both readership and popularity, for many reasons. Their layout provides an alternative way for teens to view both books and poetry. The first thing that readers may notice is that the physicality of novels in verse is strikingly different from that of traditional prose novels. With substantially more white space, fewer words per page, and font that may vary in size, style, or format, the design certainly catches the reader's eye. This is especially important for readers who may be intimidated by too many words on the page. Teens who previously were turned off by books an inch thick may find verse novels more manageable and comfortable to read. A huge benefit of this is that the readers will experience a boost in self-esteem and an increased willingness to read more.

Voice

The voice in a verse novel is generally not an external narrative, but is told as narration from the main or central character in a conversational tone. Shorter lines often take on a rhythmic effect. Mike Cadden (2011, 22) states that "there is a focus on the rhythms of the character's spoken voice that does ask the reader to 'hear' the speaker." As the voice of the narrator unfolds page by page, verse by verse, points of view are expressed colloquially, often addressing deep and intense topics. "Because of the immediate and visceral nature of poetry, many authors utilize the genre when dealing with extremely emotional topics" (Letcher 2010, 87). This, combined with the raw and gritty aspect of the voice, can engage teen readers from many walks of life. "What verse novels do is invite imaginative speculation about the things that are left unsaid by either characters or absent narrators—the descriptions of characters, settings, movements, and background information provided in the traditional prose novel that here are gaps, white or negative spaces, silences" (Cadden 2011, 24). This is a beautiful amalgamation of the literal white space on the page as a silence to be filled by the imagination of the reader. Similar to a screenplay, the space on the page of a verse novel leaves visual elements to the mind of the reader, staging the descriptions, almost as if the reader is the director of a movie, bringing her or his own personal imagery to life.

Author Terry Farish has had many discussions with teens, librarians, and teachers who have asked her, "Why verse?" She encouraged them to come up with their own theories, which resulted in the following responses:

- "The verses are like tweets—a short form that our brains are adapting to."
- "The story is told in images, and it's like you're seeing frames in a movie."
- "The length of the lines of the verses shaped the strands of a braid."
- "The lines made me read slowly."
- "The lines made me race."

Farish (2013, 33) states that she loves it when readers do this—take the book and make it theirs. Find more from Farish in the Author/Title Index.

Diversity in Verse

Rudine Sims Bishop's essay, "Windows, Mirrors, and Sliding Glass Doors" (1990, 9), is referred to frequently when addressing diversity in literature. She details the ways in which reading can be self-affirming:

Books are sometimes windows, offering views of worlds that may be real or imagined, familiar or strange. These windows are also sliding glass doors, and readers have only to walk through in imagination to become part of whatever world has been created or recreated by the author. When lighting conditions are just right, however, a window can also be a mirror. Literature transforms human experience and reflects it back to us, and in that reflection, we can see our own lives and experiences as part of the larger human experience. Reading, then, becomes a means of self-affirmation, and readers often seek their mirrors in books.

Another behemoth in the literary world is Walter Dean Myers. He has written several novels in verse, as well as an essay in *The New York Times* (2014) entitled, "Where Are the People of Color in Children's Books?" He states that after reading James Baldwin's story "Sonny's Blues" (1957), he was struck by the fact that it humanized people who were like him. "Thousands of young people have come to me saying that they love my books for some reason or the other, but I strongly suspect that what they have found in my pages is the same thing I found in 'Sonny's Blues.' They have been struck by the recognition of themselves in the story, a validation of their existence as human beings, an acknowledgment of their value by someone who understands who they are. It is the shock of recognition at its highest level" (Myers 2014). Myers states that while working in a personnel office years ago, he saw racism within the hiring practices regarding equally qualified candidates. He continues, "Books transmit values. They explore our common humanity. What is the message when some children are not represented in those books? Where are the future white personnel managers going to get their ideas of people of color? Where are the future white loan officers and future white politicians going to get their knowledge of people of color? Where are black children going to get a sense of who they are and what they can be?"

Perspectives of marginalized teens have increased the popularity of novels in verse. Sandra Hughes-Hassell defines marginalized communities as communities that:

- Have been traditionally relegated to an unimportant or powerless position in the United States.
- Systematically experience discrimination in education, employment, housing, and the judicial system.
- Include youth of color (Black/African-American, Asian, Latinx, biracial/ multiracial), Native or Indigenous youth, immigrant and refugee youth, LGBTQ+ youth, and youth with disabilities). (2017, slide 4)

I would apply a fluidity to this latter definition, as more marginalized communities may be added, such as people of Muslim and Jewish faith, etc.

Mirror books can validate the existence and lived experiences of marginalized youth by providing a counterstory to the single narrative of the dominant culture. They may also help provide positive racial identity development and healing from the damages that racism causes. Additionally, window books help readers from the dominant culture develop an appreciation and shared understanding of the contributions of marginalized communities, both as a society and to the whole world. Having a diversity of books for all kinds of youth helps to support development in a prosocial manner and "provide a forum for youth to talk about race ethnicity, gender identification, sexual orientation, and disability in a transformative way" (Hughes-Hassell 2017, slide 7).

Because the voices in verse novels provide unique and powerful perspectives, teens may develop newfound empathy. Vezzali, Stathi, and Giovannini (2012) showed that students who read stories with protagonists from other cultures showed more empathy and were more critical of prejudice toward immigrants than others who read books without intercultural themes.

Resist Using a Singular Narrative

Sandra Hughes-Hassell describes multicultural young adult literature as a form of counterstorytelling. She believes that this tool can serve multiple purposes for young adults (Hughes-Hassell 2013, 215):

- "It gives voice to teens whose voices have gone unheard and whose lives are at best underrepresented, but more often misrepresented, in the mainstream discourse."
- It challenges the single story, providing "a powerful space of affirmation and validation" (Buehler 2010, 43).
- "It presents the complexity of racial and ethnic identity formation."
- "It challenges readers whose lives have been shaped by race and privilege to consider how the world looks to groups of people that have traditionally been marginalized and oppressed, raising awareness of the inequalities those individuals face on a daily basis."

Dr. Kim Parker also recommends avoiding single-story narratives. Parker provides her students with Chimamanda Ngozi Adichie's TED Talk, "The Danger of a Single Story." When they discuss this afterward, "What sticks with my students is when Adichie explains 'The single story creates stereotypes, and the problem with stereotypes is not that they are untrue, but that they are incomplete. They make one story become the only story'" (Parker 2014, 16).

Teacher Tricia Ebarvia (2019, 41, italics in original) also finds counterstories to be a powerful resource in fighting bias and hate: "We have stories.

The stories—and more important, the *counter*-stories, the *counter-narratives*—that we choose to share with students are instrumental in helping all our students to be seen and heard, appreciated and understood. This is especially critical for students from communities whose stories are too often oversimplified, misrepresented, or rendered invisible in the dominant culture and mainstream media." The types of solidarity that can prevent or counteract bias and hate in schools can be boosted by helping foster community via centering and amplifying perspectives of marginalized populations.

Scan this QR code to view Chimamanda Ngozi Adichie's TED Talk, "The Danger of a Single Story" (2009). https://www.ted.com/talks/chimamanda_adichie_the_danger_of_a_single_story?language=en

One example of a counterstory in verse is told in *Bronx Masquerade* by Nikki Grimes, where she relates the concept of white privilege via her character Tyrone, a Black male teen (Grimes 2002, 8):

> White folks! Who they think they kidding? They might as well go blow smoke up somebody else's you-know-what, 'cause a Black man's got no chance in this country. I be lucky if I make it to twenty-one with all these fools running around with AK-47s . . . Life is cold. Future? What I got is right now, right here, spending time with my homeys. Wish there was some future to talk about. I could use me some future.

This passage gives insight into Tyrone's world, which can be a mirror for some readers and an eye-opening sliding-glass door to others. This can provoke somewhat uncomfortable but healthy and insightful discussions about what it is like to be an insider versus what it is like being an outsider.

Author Jason Reynolds advocates for proactive discussions like these. "We should talk to them about everything. We should be leading these conversations . . . we need to use the terms and words, and recognize that not all conversations need to be about trauma, but address everyday life. It's important that we lead . . . most of the time, the adults are more scared of difficult conversations than the kids are" (First Book 2019). His copanelist,

Scan this QR code to view the full video of Reynolds and Woodson's discussion at the 2019 *Antiracist Book Festival* at American University (First Book 2019). https://www.facebook.com/FirstBook/videos/336735357198385

author Jacqueline Woodson, concurs. "Adult shame is what affects conversations, not kids" (First Book 2019). For more from Nikki Grimes, Jason Reynolds, and Jacqueline Woodson, see the Author/Title Index.

Another example of a counterstory within a novel in verse is *Saving Red* by Sonya Sones. The protagonist, Molly, searches the streets for homeless people for a school assignment. One girl, Red, stands out to her. Molly quickly realizes that Red appears to be mentally ill and there is a lot more to her story than homelessness alone. This is a terrific springboard to discussions about mental health with teens, and a mirror for those who need to find some of their own characteristics in books. What appears to be posttraumatic stress disorder (PTSD), bipolar disorder, and schizophrenia are all addressed via multiple characters. To find more about *Saving Red*, go to the Author/Title Index.

Beverly Tatum's ABC framework of inclusive learning (Ask, Bridge, Cultivate) requires scrutinizing youth literacy and identity (Tatum 2000). This is detailed further by Kumasi and Hughes-Hassell (2017, 16), as they extend it with a critical lens, adding these important questions:

> "A—Ask: Who is left out of the picture in our collections and services . . . who is being misrepresented or under-represented in our services and resources?
>
> B—Bridge: How might we bridge the disconnects for those whose voices and cultures are missing or underrepresented in our services and resources?
>
> C—Cultivate: How might we cultivate new voices or be agents of change who challenge the status quo?"

As noted in Jewett (2017), "If what we read forms group identity and defines common values, and if what we read excludes stories by and about people of color, then is it no surprise that as a culture we do not identify with or value the bodies and minds of people of color." Jewett continues by wondering if Trayvon Martin might still be alive if George Zimmerman had read books by and about Black people in high school. Additionally, she ponders if reading such books may have affected the verdict in Zimmerman's murder trial, resulting in a conviction, if the jurors on the case had read them.

We Need Diverse Books

We Need Diverse Books (WNDB) is a grassroots, nonprofit organization of lovers of children's books that advocates for important changes in the publishing industry to produce and promote literature that authentically reflects and honors the lives of all young people. Founded in 2014, the mission of WNDB is to put more books featuring diverse characters into the hands of all children. Its main goal of creating a world where all children can see themselves in books is reflective of Dr. Rudine Sims Bishop's mirrors, windows, and sliding-glass doors metaphor (1990).

WNDB defines diversity as follows (WNDB 2019):

We recognize all diverse experiences, including (but not limited to) LGBTQIA, Native, people of color, gender diversity, people with disabilities*, and ethnic, cultural, and religious minorities.* We subscribe to a broad definition of disability, which includes but is not limited to physical, sensory, cognitive, intellectual, or developmental disabilities, chronic conditions, and mental illnesses (this may also include addiction). Furthermore, we subscribe to a social model of disability, which presents disability as created by barriers in the social environment, due to lack of equal access, stereotyping, and other forms of marginalizations.

(Note that the asterisks, in the original text, were used to denote that a broader definition of disabilities and minorities is being used.)

Since the group's inception, cofounder, chief executive officer (CEO), and president Ellen Oh has endeavored to expand WNDB to include many author advocates. Some of these include chief operating officer (COO) Dhonielle Clayton, Lamar Giles, Sona Charaipotra, Alex Gino, Cynthia Leitich Smith, Matt de la Pena, Jacqueline Woodson, and Linda Sue Park, among many others. WNDB offers many programs and services, including the Walter Award and Walter Grant, internships, mentorships, writing awards, conference panels, and anthologies written by collaborations of diverse authors.

For more information and to obtain WNDB resources, visit https://diversebooks.org/about-wndb.

Scan this QR code for a brief video from WNDB (2014). https://youtu.be/mrrh0G-OkBw.

Cooperative Children's Book Center

The Cooperative Children's Book Center (CCBC) is a unique examination, study, and research library of the School of Education at the University of Wisconsin-Madison. The CCBC has compiled information for this post: *Publishing Statistics on Children's/YA Books About People of Color and First/Native Nations and by People of Color and First/Native Nations Authors and Illustrators.*

The inventory included 3,134 books published in 2018. For more information regarding how the statistics were compiled, visit http://ccbc.education.wisc.edu/books/pcstats.asp.

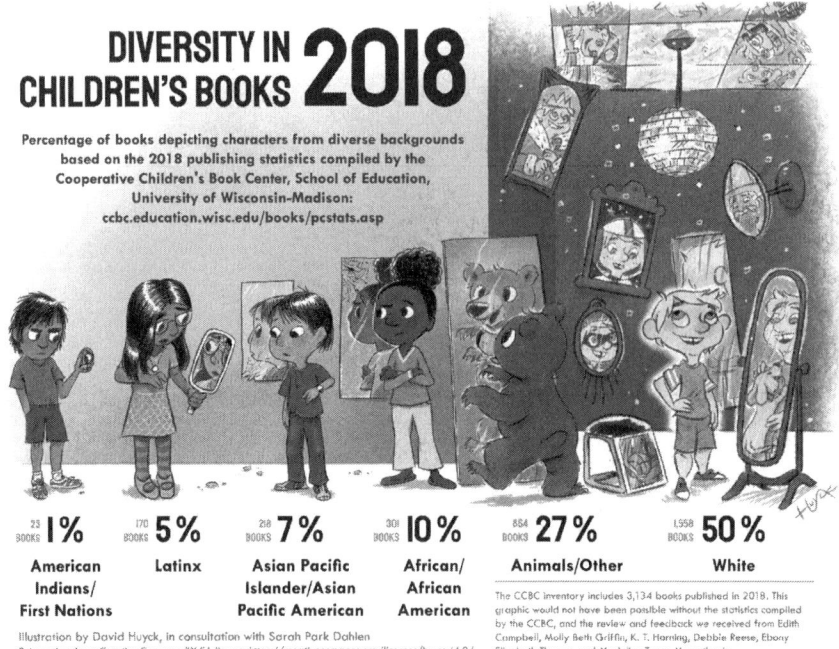

Figure 1.1 Diversity in Children's Books 2018 Source: Huyck and Dahlen (2019). Created in consultation with Edith Campbell, Molly Beth Griffin, K. T. Horning, Debbie Reese, Ebony Elizabeth Thomas, and Madeline Tyner, with statistics compiled by the Cooperative Children's Book Center, School of Education, University of Wisconsin-Madison.

In 2018, there were more books featuring animals/other than all four of the studied marginalized populations (American Indians/First Nations, Latinx, Asian Pacific Islander/Asian Pacific American, and African/African American) combined. Although this showed a slight improvement from the 2015 study, a wide disparity clearly remains when it comes to representation in children's literature. See Figure 1.1 for a graphic representation of these statistics.

While the White child in the infographic has a large, clear mirror (and even a disco ball full of mirrors) to see himself in, the size of the mirrors decreases dramatically for the marginalized children. They are also cracked, distorted, or broken, which is a metaphor for inaccuracies or harmful representations in some books. Not only do we need more representation for these children, but we need better representation. One way to do this is by selecting books written by #OwnVoices authors whenever possible. #OwnVoices authors share a diverse or marginalized trait with their main character. Evaluate books with a critical lens to see who is left out and replace books with stereotypes and harmful content with more authentic representation.

What Is a Diversity Audit?

Karen Jensen, a collection development librarian and creator of the *School Library Journal's* "Teen Librarian Toolbox," has worked extensively with diversity audits (see Jensen 2017). A diversity audit involves counting the titles in your collection to determine percentages of representation in specific collection categories. This holds the creators of the collection accountable for assessing and developing a collection inclusive of something other than the traditionally dominant voice (i.e., White, cisgender, heterosexual, able-bodied male). Remember that diversity is not just about race—it includes marginalizations of all kinds.

Jensen states, "Eighty percent of librarianship is made up of forty-year-old white women, like me. We each go into collection development with our own biases and privilege, which can influence purchasing. Statistics put the science back in library science. Identifying and filling gaps for inclusive collections promotes learning, engagement, compassion, and a more authentic world citizenship" (2019b, slide 5).

If the thought of a large audit is overwhelming, Jensen suggests tackling it via a reverse diversity audit: "Pick the topics you want to audit. Find recent, reputable book lists for that topic. Check to see how many of the titles you have in your collection. Fill holes accordingly . . . develop a schedule to be sure you look at each topic over the course of a year" (2019b, slide 10). For more detailed resources about diversity audits, visit Jensen's blog at http://www.teenlibrariantoolbox.com /files/2017/11/Diversity-Audit-Outline-2017-with-Sources.pdf.

> Although there are several ways to conduct an audit, one option is to start with a questionnaire such as this one, provided by Lee and Low Books (2017). https://www.leeandlow.com /uploads/loaded_document/408 /Classroom-Library-Questionnaire _FINAL.pdf.
>
>

How Do Novels in Verse Fit Into All of This?

Verse novels address a widely diverse demographic and array of tough topics, as well as celebrating other interests. These include but are not limited to:

- Varied cultures
- Varied religions
- Racism
- Prejudice
- LGBTQ+

- Mental illness
- Black Lives Matter
- Gun violence
- Poverty
- Homelessness

- Sexual assault
- Self-harm/suicide
- Domestic violence
- Family dynamics
- Adoption
- Family secrets
- First love/sex
- Addiction/alcoholism
- Disabilities
- Bullying
- Immigrants
- Refugees

- English-language learners (ELLs)
- Writing
- Performing arts
- Music
- Sports
- Empowerment
- Recovery
- Therapy
- Dancing
- College
- Coming of age
- Resilience

Sylvia M. Vardell also touts the value of diverse viewpoints via poetry. Authors of novels in verse show teen readers how the human landscape is both fascinating and robust by showing both differences *and* similarities among each other. Cultures, language, and experiences are used by poets in compelling ways because poetry is so succinct. "Sometimes powerful points about prejudice, identity, and cultural conflict can be made in very few words. In addition, we can also rediscover our human universality in poems' words and feelings, which cross cultural boundaries" (Vardell 2015a, 27). A perfect example of this is Elizabeth Acevedo's verse novel, *The Poet X*, which has earned numerous awards, including the 2019 Michael L. Printz Award for Excellence in Young Adult Literature, the 2019 Pura Belpre Award, for Latinx authors affirming the Latinx experience; and the 2018 National Book Award. See the Author/Title Index for more from Elizabeth Acevedo.

What Types of Books in Verse are There?

The phrases *novels in verse* and *verse novels* are used primarily in this book because most of the forthcoming books in this guide are fiction selections. However, documentary novels in verse (generally historical fiction) and memoirs in verse can also provide those windows, mirrors, and sliding-glass doors (Bishop 1990), that teachers and librarians should be offering their teens. One big question is: What is the difference between a book of poems and a novel in verse? People sometimes use the terms interchangeably, but they are actually different. A poetry book includes poems that are separate from each other, whereas a novel in verse uses those poems to tell one continuing story. Think of it this way: Poetry books hold collections of poems, while novels in verse contain poems that progress to reveal the narrative of a complete story.

There is some dispute among libraries as to the genre of novels in verse. Should they be shelved in the fiction section or in poetry? Campbell (2004, 615), explains that "the structure of a verse novel . . . can be quite different from the novel, which is built with rising conflict toward a climax, followed by a denouement. The verse novel is often more like a wheel, with the hub a compelling emotional event, and the narration referring to this event like the spokes." Cadden (2011) sees this intersection as a golden opportunity to provide gateways for readers who otherwise may not approach a particular genre. Using verse novels may help students develop an appreciation for other genre crossovers, too. Teens who previously may never have picked up poetry may find it more accessible after reading novels in verse.

> Scan this QR code for a brief video on the genre of verse books (Horrocks 2013). https://youtu.be/LXViVD7LQAM.
>
>

In 2013, Jennie Yabroff posted on the website Biographile.com, "Memoirs . . . used to be autobiography's emotional, disreputable little sister." However, memoirs are now emerging more and more. When Jacqueline Woodson's memoir in verse, *Brown Girl Dreaming,* won the National Book Award in 2014, the tremendous level of respect for this author confirmed the fact that memoirs in verse for tweens and teens would likely be enduring for prosperity. Woodson states, "This is how memory comes to me—in small moments with all of this white space around them. I didn't think this memoir could be told any other way. It felt like it would be untrue to the story to try to write a straight narrative out of lyrical memory. Also, I felt this way best expressed what I was trying to say—that words have always been coming to me, that I've always been trying to hold on to them, set them free, floating onto the pages. This form shows them floating, shows the words moving slowly across, down, over the page" (*Poetry for Children* blog, cited in Vardell 2015b). See more on *Brown Girl Dreaming* and other memoirs in verse in the Author/Title Index and Content Tag Index.

As to the question of cataloging and shelving, experience has shown the following as being most logical for the Young Adult section:

- Books that are collections of poems belong in the 811 poetry section.
- Novels in verse, because they tell the entire narrative of a story, belong in fiction. This also enables more accessibility for teens who may be intimidated by the 811 section.
- Memoirs in verse can be shelved with autobiographies and biographies, listed alphabetically by the last name of the person that it is about. Again, this

makes them much more accessible to search by the last name of the person of interest.

- Documentary-style verse books are generally still fictionalized, similar to historical fiction, and should be shelved with fiction. (Think of books like *Loving vs. Virginia* by Patricia Hruby Powell, and Margarita Engle's *Jazz Owls*. Find more from Woodson and Engle in the Author/Title Index.)

How Can Novels in Verse Help Reluctant Readers?

First, let's begin with a brief history of Young Adult literature. Karen Jensen, in the *School Library Journal's* "Teen Librarian Toolbox," created an infographic that explains the journey (see Jensen 2019a).

S. E. Hinton wrote what has come to be known as the first Young Adult book in 1967, when she was only sixteen years old. *The Outsiders* still appears today on many high school required reading lists. The 1970s brought about the first "Golden Age" of realistic fiction for teens, with titles that included topics such as sex (*Forever,* Blume 1975) and a first-person account of using drugs (*Go Ask Alice*, Anonymous 1971). The 1980s was a period of market growth, with genre fiction moving in to replace novels focusing just on teen problems. The *Sweet Valley High* (Pascal 1983) series ran for twenty years of publication. The 1988 book *Fallen Angels* by Walter Dean Myers, depicted a coming-of-age story that takes place during the Vietnam War. R. L. Stine and Christopher Pike ruled the horror genre in the 1990s, and some teen classics, such as *Speak* (Anderson 1999) came out during that period as well. *Speak,* a story of sexual assault and finding your voice, remains relevant over twenty years later.

The "Second Golden Age" came about in the 2000s, with a 400 percent surge in the number of young adult books published. The Michael L. Printz Award for teen literature was introduced, with the first one bestowed upon Walter Dean Myers for *Monster* in 2000. Vampires and dystopian themes ruled, with Stephenie Meyer's *Twilight* series originating in 2005 and Suzanne Collins's *The Hunger Games* trilogy storming into 2008. Moving into the 2010s, more representation was requested of authors and publishers for inclusion of diverse demographics. Some popular inclusive titles during this time were *I'll Give You the Sun* by Jandy Nelson (2014); *Everything, Everything* by Nicola Yoon (2015); *The Hate U Give* by Angie Thomas (2017); and *Long Way Down* by Jason Reynolds (2017). See more from Reynolds in the Author/Title Index.

So, where do we go from here? In the past few years, librarians, authors, publishers, and readers have expressed a need for more authentic representation via #OwnVoices, as previously mentioned. Underrepresented marginalized communities, such as books written by authors of the Muslim faith, begin to be published more and more, possibly as a way of pushing back against the current political climate both in the United States and elsewhere, and raising awareness. Some of these include *Love from A to Z* by S. K. Ali (2019); and *Other Words for Home* by Jasmine Warga (2019). See more from Warga in the Author/Title Index. Because many Young Adult books have portrayed characters at the older end of high school or beginning college, the demand for more middle-grade books has increased so those kids can see themselves in books, too (Jensen 2019a).

Although their representation in books is evolving, some teens may shy away from reading. Reluctant readers might be hesitant to read for multiple reasons, including:

- They are struggling readers.
- They have dyslexia/other learning disabilities.
- Lack of confidence.
- ELLs.
- They think reading isn't "cool."
- They haven't yet found books they identify with.
- Matching the right book to the reader can be challenging.

Figure 1.2 A Brief History of Young Adult Literature Reprinted with permission of Karen Jensen.

Novels in verse present ways of addressing many of these reasons. First, compared to a regular prose novel, verse novels may have about half the number of words per page. When readers who are struggling, have dyslexia or another disability, haven't spent much time with books, are learning the English language, or are not confident in their reading are handed a novel in verse, the white space has huge appeal for them. Reading a whole novel in verse can make a reluctant reader feel successful, boosting their confidence and encouraging them to read more in the future. Blay and Brown (2019) say, "Students who hesitate to read in general may perhaps bring a level of interest, given a more accessible text . . ."

Dorie Raybuck (2015) states that many reluctant readers are visual readers, so the placement of the font on the page is appealing and adds to the imagery. She goes on to state that kinesthetic and auditory learners also identify with poetry by feeling and hearing, as verse tends to have a rhythm. Former Young People's Poet Laureate, author Margarita Engle refers to this rhythm as the "hoofbeat" in poetry (Farish 2013). See more from Margarita Engle by turning to the Author/Title Index.

Going back to the "director of the movie" metaphor, the imagery in a verse novel is vivid, and the graphic placement of words on the page contributes to the understanding and rhythm of the words. Kwame Alexander demonstrates a great mastery of this skill in his books. *The Crossover* (2014), *Rebound* (2018), and *Booked* (2016), in particular, have a tremendous amount of graphic effects in the font type and placement, which makes them particularly rhythmic. See more on Alexander's books in the Author/Title Index.

In addition to struggling readers and readers with dyslexia or a reading disability, many reluctant readers may be those who haven't yet seen themselves in a book via mirrors, windows, or sliding doors (Bishop 1990). When we give teens who are reluctant readers diverse books that reflect their own lives or books that give a perspective into a marginalized person's life, we open those mirrors, windows, and sliding doors right up. Sharon Flake states, "Black boys will read. But to get them off to a flying start, we've got to give them books that remind them of home—who they are. When this happens, they fly through books—even the most challenged readers. They hunger for the work like a homeless man finally getting a meal that's weeks overdue" (Flake 2007, 14).

If we expect to reach reluctant readers with books, we cannot stereotype them. The interests of reluctant readers vary as widely as those of teens who love to read. Fortunately, novels in verse cover a wide breadth of interests, genres, specific attributes, and situations.

The Young Adult Library Services Association (YALSA) has a selection committee that creates a list of Quick Picks for Reluctant Young Adult Readers. This team is appointed annually and is made up of library professionals who service teens. These professionals are charged with reading and evaluating teen books in order to create annual selection lists that recommend quality, accessible choices for reluctant readers. Teachers and librarians can use this list to assist with collection development and creating readers' advisories for reluctant readers. The YALSA criteria for this list is described in the next section.

Reluctant Young Adult Readers Selection Criteria

Note: These criteria are only meant as suggestions for evaluating a book. Not all criteria may fit all books.

1. **Physical appearance**
   - Cover—catchy, action-oriented, attractive, appealing, with a good "blurb"
   - Print style—sufficiently large for enjoyable reading

- Format—an appropriate and appealing balance of text and white space
- Artwork/illustrations—enticing, realistic, demonstrating diversity

2. **Style**
   - Clear writing that communicates without long, convoluted sentences of sophisticated vocabulary
   - Acceptable literary quality and effectiveness of presentation
   - Simple vocabulary, but not noticeably controlled

3. **Fiction**
   - High-interest "hook" in the first ten pages
   - Well-defined characters
   - Sufficient plot to sustain interest
   - Plot lines developed through dialogue and action
   - Familiar themes that have emotional appeal for teenagers
   - Believable treatment
   - Single point of view
   - Touches of humor when appropriate
   - Chronological order

4. **Informational books**
   - Technical language acceptable if defined in context
   - Accuracy
   - Objectivity

     (Quick Picks for Reluctant Young Adult Readers Selection Criteria is used with permission of the Young Adult Library Services Association, a division of the American Library Association.)

Again, not all books meet every single criterion These are guidelines for the selected lists, not an exclusive list of all books that may reach reluctant readers.

Many facets of these criteria are present in novels in verse. Visit http://www.ala.org/yalsa/quick-picks-reluctant-young-adult-readers to view the current list of nominees, the current picks, as well as those from past years. Please note that this does not mean that every novel in verse suggested in this book would qualify for a Quick Picks for Reluctant Readers selected list, just that many novels in verse are also accessible to reluctant readers.

English Language Learners can also benefit from the verse novel format, which can help them become more comfortable with reading, writing, and speaking English. Terry Farish works with ELL students. She seeks out accessible novels that contain "stories that can build a bridge from the known to the less known. I look for books that explore U.S. culture for new Americans, as well as ones about a student's own culture . . . many who work with English language learners and others who struggle with reading seek novels that promote fluency and a sense of competence in readers. Verse novels accomplish just that. They can move fast and offer readers at any level a feeling of completion" (Farish 2013, 33).

Amy L. Freyn, Ed.D, has written about her research on using poetry with ELL students in the *Journal of Education and Practice* (Freyn 2017). She found that a meaningful language-learning experience can be accomplished by teaching poetry in the language classroom. V. K. Pushpa and S. Y. Savaedi (2014) concur that by using the appropriate teaching strategies, students may be more interested and motivated, therefore communicating more and promoting better learning of the English language; and poetry is an authentic and valuable resource for teaching ELLs.

As Farish was working on her book *The Good Braider* (2012), she wanted to home in on the truth and specificity of the story. She found that poetry provided the spareness with specificity that she was seeking. During the 2013 Association of Writers and Writing Programs (AWP) Conference, Rita Dove, Poet Laureate Consultant to the Library of Congress (1993–1995), participated in a panel entitled "Staggered Tellings: Immediacy, Intimacy, and Ellipses in the Verse Novel." She stated, "Verse novels offer the weight of each word, the weight of the sentence, the weight of the line, the weight of white space, heightened attention to sound, and deep allegiance to silence" (Barker, Clark, Dove, Galassi, and Young 2013).

Whether struggling readers, teens who haven't yet seen themselves reflected in books, or ELLs, asking questions is key. Providing a strong readers' advisory, including novels in verse that include a wide variety of topics, demographics, and styles, will help match books to readers. Raybuck (2015) says, "The reluctant reader cannot be stereotyped if we expect to reach him or her with a good read. Reluctant readers are as varied in interests as those who love to read, and luckily novels in verse come in many genres, both fiction and nonfiction."

Advocacy and Rethinking the Canon

Many schools have required reading lists for their students. These are often made up of books considered "classics" that have been around for many years. Some may still have some value for use, but others are outdated (and perhaps even downright harmful and offensive). Novels in verse can provide a valid replacement or pairing for some canonical texts.

Definitions of Canon

Canon: n., from the Latin canon or "rule." Originally, an ecclesiastical code of law or standard of judgment, usually based upon determinate set of authorized texts, like the canonical books of the Bible, Torah, Qu'ran, or Sutras (Retrieved from http://faculty.goucher.edu/eng211/canon_of_english_literature.htm.)

An authoritative list of books accepted as Holy Scripture (Merriam-Webster, 2019.)

It has been argued that until literature is "canon," it has not risen to the level of sophistication where it could be seriously studied by scholars. However, the reverse can also be true. Canonization often introduces predictable biases, which distorts the literature. The "authoritative list of books" as canon tends to marginalize the powerless and favor the powerful, regardless of the merit of the work (Goucher College n.d.).

Problematic Texts

Unfortunately, many texts considered canon are outdated in general or include outdated representations. Dr. Ebony Elizabeth Thomas, associate professor in the Literacy, Culture, and International Educational Division at the University of Pennsylvania's Graduate School of Education, has widely examined texts for problematic content. Thomas uses *To Kill a Mockingbird* as an example of a classic book that needs connections to be made with students' modern experiences in today's world. She suggests that every teacher ask these three key questions when considering using this book:

1. "What kind of students do I have?" (Thomas, Reese, and Lesesne 2015, 68)

    This could include things such as the demographic makeup of the group and whether the dynamics of the setting (classroom, library, etc.) emphasize competition, community, or both.

2. "How can I contextualize/historicize [this book] for my students?" (Thomas et al. 2015, 69)

    Thomas stresses the importance of performing analysis such as this before attempting to teach any classic literature, particularly literature about race. Educators also need to realize that today's high school students were born after the tragic events of September 11, 2001. Scaffolding the history represented in books with multimedia resources can show varied points in time and also represent different viewpoints.

3. "How can I illustrate the contemporary relevance of [this book] to my students?" (Thomas et al. 2015, 69)

    Thomas encourages events happening in local, national, and world news be brought into the classroom. Teens are aware of the discussions happening in politics, current events, and by extension, some pop culture environments. This can be applied to compare/contrast with the book.

Dr. Debbie Reese, who is tribally enrolled at Nambe Pueblo, New Mexico, is a scholar who works to continuously evaluate and advocate for authentic Native voices in children's literature. "At my site, *American Indians in Children's Literature*, teachers will find my lists of recommended books as well as in-depth discussions of books I like and those I find problematic. Many people write to say that such critiques are especially useful at helping them see bias and error that usually go unnoticed or unremarked upon by reviewers in mainstream journals" (Thomas et al. 2015, 71).

Reese has enforced much advocacy regarding not using *Little House on the Prairie* in the classroom. Thomas, Reese, and Lesesne (2015, 70) give the following example:

> The teacher is reading aloud from *Little House on the Prairie* and comes to that part where she'll read, "The only good Indian is a dead Indian." What will the teacher do? . . . Someone [the child] likely trusts and respects has just read out loud a horrible sentence. It'll happen three more times . . . consider how might a Native child perform on that spelling test, having just heard that "the only good Indian is a dead Indian?"

Reese's dedication to this work resulted in the award previously known as the Wilder Medal between 1960 and 2017 undergoing a name change, to the Children's Literature Legacy Award, in 2018 (Association for Library Services to Children 2018). Reese stated, "Immersed in a world that so pervasively stereotypes 'other,' it can be difficult for anyone to see the stereotypes at all. That pervasiveness also makes it hard to step outside that space and look critically at what we believe we know about other cultures" (Thomas et al. 2015, 71).

For more information from Reese's blog regarding *Little House on the Prairie* and other book criticisms, recommendations, and discussions, visit https://americanindiansinchildrensliterature.blogspot.com. Additionally, Dr. Reese has adapted the book *An Indigenous Peoples' History of the United States for Young People* (Dunbar-Ortiz 2019), with Jean Mendoza (adapter).

Thomas (2013) has expressed concerns regarding Black children and other characters of color portrayed often as in trouble or suffering:

> Stories of oppression and inequality are important ones that must be told and retold. Nevertheless, those of us tasks with presenting these texts to young people would do well to consider the impressions of African American children and youth they might be left with if the majority of the Black American characters they encounter are enslaved, suffering under Jim Crow, living under duress during the Civil Rights Movement, and/or struggling to survive the nation's postmodern inner cities. If there are few (or zero) young African American detectives, doctors, crime fighters, superheroes,

brave soldiers and knights, or princesses in our stories, what ideas about the humanity, the diversity within, and the inherent worth might young people from other cultures take away from their readings? What might Black kids and teens themselves come to believe about their inherent worth. How does this affect the development of young readers' imaginations, dreams, and aspirations?

Continuous learning is encouraged by Thomas for teachers, librarians, and mentors of youth. She recommends joining the Assembly on Literature for Adolescents (ALAN) and YALSA, attending conferences for professional development, and participating in social media discussions.

For more information and resources from Dr. Thomas, visit her blog at http://thedarkfantastic.blogspot.com. Thomas also recently released her book *The Dark Fantastic: Race and the Imagination from Harry Potter to the Hunger Games* (2019).

Empathy

Novels in verse provide excellent opportunities for building empathy via their representation and voice. Students are expressing less interest in some canonical texts. In particular, linguistically and culturally diverse teens may not consider canon relevant to the experiences in their lives. They may have difficulty connecting to subjects that they find inaccessible. "Students who hesitate to read in general may perhaps bring a level of interest if given a more accessible text" (Blay and Brown 2019).

Knowing that reading creates empathy, reading the canon through four years of high school results in missed opportunities for exposure and understanding of nonwhite perspectives. "Racism is not about a single person as much as it is about a system of privilege and discrimination," according to Ebarvia (2018). When she saw white nationalists marching in Charlottesville, Ebarvia thought about the fact that each one of those people full of hatred had at one time been students in our classrooms. "If we are not being intentionally anti-racist in our curricular and instructional choices, I'm not sure what we're doing in the classroom" (Ebarvia 2018a).

During the *School Library Journal*'s 2019 SLJteenLive Virtual Summit, Cassy Lee presented a segment of a session on "Fostering Empathy Through Library Programming and Collaboration." Lee, the Learning Center coordinator at the Chinese American International School in San Francisco, shared information about building a "Human Library." This library is designed to "build a positive framework for conversations that can challenge stereotypes and prejudices through dialogue. The Human Library is a place where real people are on loan to readers. A place where difficult questions are expected, appreciated, and answered" (Lee 2019). Part of the Human Library project includes embedding social justice and equity issues into teacher/librarian collaborations, to afford students with choices and voices to empower them.

Comments from students included, from a sixth grader, "She is Muslim but lives in a society where most people are white and Christian, and I could relate to her because we were both 'different.' I now understand how although some people look different, we are all similar." An eighth grader commented, "I'm also multiracial and half Asian, but people don't usually think I'm Asian. I understand that a person's ethnicity can be different from how they look." Lee also suggests book clubs, displays of diverse literature, author visits, and book drives as tools that can promote empathy. She urges teachers and librarians to never stop learning and growing, attend conferences and programs, and encourage others to grow with you.

#DisruptTexts

#DisruptTexts is a grassroots, crowdfunded effort created by teachers, for teachers, to challenge the traditional canon. Its goal is to create a more inclusive, representative, and equitable curriculum for students. Part of its mission is to assist and develop teachers committed to practices of anti-racist/anti-bias teaching. According to Ebarvia (2019), "If we are people committed to equity, then we must understand our role in these systems and how we might disrupt them. So diversify the curriculum, yes, but let's not stop there."

Each Monday on Twitter, there is a #DisruptTexts chat at 8 a.m. EST. Teachers all across the country (and even the world) come together online to apply a critical lens to a specified text. The #DisruptTexts chat and website are facilitated by Tricia Ebarvia, Lorena German, Dr. Kim Parker, and Julia Torres. Some of the books that they have disrupted include *The Great Gatsby, To Kill a Mockingbird, Lord of the Flies,* and *The Crucible.* Ebarvia (2018a) says:

> When we disrupt texts, we can be honest about ALL of our literary history, which must include more voices. This isn't rewriting history; it's correcting it.

For more information about #DisruptTexts and the facilitators, visit the following sites:

https://disrupttexts.org
https://triciaebarvia.org
https://drkimparker.org
https://juliaetorres.blog
http://multiculturalclassroomconsulting.com

The National Council of Teachers of English (NCTE) has resources available for developing rationales for using specific texts, as well as guidance for reporting censorship. For more information, visit http://www.ncte.org/action /anti-censorship/rationales.

Decolonizing the Canon

Teacher Christina Torres stresses the power of words like *classics* and *canon,* and how they send a message that voices from marginalized communities are not worthy of the same praise or study: "Our students deserve to know that their voices and powerful voices from the communities they come from are as brilliant and worthy as we have been pushed to read for generations before. This is important work not ONLY in communities of color—where students need their identities validated and uplifted in a world that continually tries to oppress and other them—but in majority-white classrooms as well" (Torres 2019). This brings us back to providing counterstories to the single-story narratives that society has given regarding Black, Indigenous, Latinx, LGBTQ+, and other communities that have been historically silenced (Jewett 2017):

> Decolonizing the canon would, as the authors propose, reverse the "prejudice, stereotyping, discrimination, and biases that are embedded within the ELA curriculum" while teaching students "deeper compassion, elevated sympathies, and greater acceptance" for people of color.

Here are some examples of some novels in verse used to disrupt and rethink the canon:

Canon = *Romeo and Juliet* by William Shakespeare
Novel in verse = *Street Love* by Walter Dean Myers

Canon = *The House on Mango Street* by Sandra Cisneros
Novel in verse = *The Poet X* by Elizabeth Acevedo

Workshopping the Canon

Both readability and relatability can be a struggle for students and teachers regarding classical works of literature. We already know that no single text is appropriate for all high school and middle school students due to their varying strengths, interests, and possible challenges. Verse novels offer accessibility and representation that works of the canon often do not. However, many school districts still require books considered canon. Mary Styslinger, associate professor of English and literacy education at the University of South Carolina, promotes finding ways to interweave literature with literacy, a process that she refers to as "workshopping the canon." She uses the term *workshop* as a verb, meaning that it involves teachers taking action. "When we workshop the canon, we actively and purposefully partner classical texts with a variety of high-interest, multiple genres within a reading and writing workshop structure, aligning the teaching of literature with what we have come to recognize as best practices in the teaching of literacy" (Styslinger 2017, xii).

So, should we teach works of canon or not? Many teachers bounce back and forth between teaching both young adult novels and classic novels, often due to the expectations of school districts, parents, standards, students, and the self. Styslinger (2017, 3) continues:

> No matter your position, if we want students to read more often and subsequently improve their reading proficiency, then we need to provide high-interest and more accessible texts. We need to better incorporate what students are more likely to read out of school into the school curriculum. We need to surround students with all kinds of relatable genres. At the same time, some teachers or districts may find it hard to let go of a number of great works of literature . . . Workshopping structures and strategies enable teachers to interweave other genres as a means of providing students with more accessible text and diverse cultural representations, bridging the gap between out of school and in-school reading.

An extensive survey conducted by Beers and Probst (2013), cited by Styslinger (2017), determines that the most frequent listings for books taught in grades 9–10 include *To Kill a Mockingbird, The Adventures of Huckleberry Finn, The Scarlet Letter*, and *Romeo and Juliet.* Styslinger acknowledges valid arguments both for and against teaching works from the canon. She cites Bloom (1994) as supporting the canon and using those texts as a basis for comparison, as well as those challenging texts of the canon for their singular Eurocentric, masculine representations. Most notable is the absence of African American, Native American, Asian American, Latinx, and female representations of understanding and authors from these groups (Baker 1980; Barker 1989; Bruchac 1987; Ling 1990, cited in Styslinger 2017).

Weaver (2002, cited in Styslinger 2017), found that the instructional approaches that we use when reading and teaching in class mold students as readers. In other words, students' definitions of reading are shaped by teachers' definitions of reading. Again, this goes back to the idea of a singular narrative. Styslinger continues by discussing how readers are shaped by teachers, and not always for the better. She cites Atwell's (1998) foundational text on workshopping, "Twenty-One Lessons Teachers Demonstrate About Reading" (28–29):

- Reading is a serious, painful business.
- Literature is even more serious and painful, not to mention boring.
- Reading is a performance for an audience of one: the teacher.

- There is one interpretation of a text: the teacher's (or that of the teacher's manual).
- Reading requires memorization and mastery of information, terms, definitions, and theories.
- Reading is followed by a test.
- You learn about literature by listening to teachers talk about it.
- Teachers talk a lot about literature, but teachers don't read.
- Reading is a waste of English class time.

So, how do we keep students engaged? Fostering classrooms with responsive environments is a great place to start, with connections to real-life, relatable experiences. "Monocultural approaches to teaching increase the achievement gap and augment adolescents; disengagement with literacy. When we teach one text at a time, we limit perspectives. Only one voice is heard" (NCTE 2007, cited in Styslinger 2017). Again, the single narratives must be replaced by counterstories, using a critical lens (Hughes-Hassell 2013; Ebarvia 2019).

Many of these counterstories are present in the novels in verse presented in Part Two, "Readers' Advisory and Activities." Teachers and librarians can also explore the Content Tag Index in the back of this book for specific demographics, needs, and interests, so as to best match readers to books. Then students can read, write, and discuss their creative writing with others in order to further engage them and provide multiple perspectives to them.

Conclusion

Novels in verse are an accessible way to reach marginalized teens and reluctant readers for many reasons. These include white space, voice, rhythm, topics, and representation of diverse populations of all kinds. They can help provide a counterstory to the single narrative. Verse novels can help build empathy and encourage engaging with the text via written and spoken poetry activities. Teachers and librarians should use a critical lens to examine the texts that they are using with students for problematic content.

Disrupting texts and rethinking the canon can help provide a more authentic and relatable experience for teens. Librarians and teachers can promote novels in verse by putting them on display and book-talking them just like any other novel. Their themes and representation have strong appeal and the ability to hook readers quickly once they open the books. The next section provides a readers' advisory and activities for using novels in verse with teens.

PART TWO

Readers' Advisory and Activities

Now for the fun part—the books and activities! This hefty section is packed with plenty of options to meet the interests of a wide variety of teens. Each book listed contains bibliographical information, grade-level advisories, content tags, and a brief summary. The content tags, in particular, will aid librarians and teachers in helping place the right books into teens' hands.

The novels in verse are arranged alphabetically by the authors' last names. They are also indexed in the back of the book by both author and content tags in order to assist teachers and librarians in quickly finding what they need for each student. Suggested activities are provided for the books that can be used as entire classroom activities or for individual students, depending on needs. Whenever possible, novels in verse written by #OwnVoices authors were used. There is a verse novel desert of sorts in some forms of representation. While researching for this book, I found Indigenous, Muslim, transgender, and nonbinary representation in particular to have little to no #OwnVoices representation in verse novels. This means that there is a wide opportunity for authors and publishers to create novels in verse for these marginalized communities in particular. Author Eric Gansworth, an enrolled member of the Anondaga Nation, is currently working on a memoir in verse. This welcome addition to the verse format is entitled *Apple: Skin to the Core*, which is scheduled to be released in fall 2020 from Levine Querido.

Please note that most of the poetry activities suggested are based upon poetic forms, not poetic devices. This was done intentionally so that teachers and librarians could include the devices based upon the needs of their students and requirements of the curriculum. A Glossary of Poetic Devices is provided in the back of the book as well. Common Core State Standards (CCSS) and American Association of School Librarians (AASL) Standards

Framework information are also provided for each activity, so that inserting the activities into lesson planning can be done easily.

The Poet X by Elizabeth Acevedo
HarperTeen
March 6, 2018
ISBN: 978-0062662804

Grades: 7 and up

Content Tags:
body image, Catholicism, dating, Dominican, family dynamics, immigrants, Latinx, LGBTQ+, open mic, religion, slam poetry, teachers, twins

Summary

Xiomara Batista is growing up in Harlem in a strict Dominican Catholic family. She often feels that she has no voice in choosing what her life will be. The decisions in her life have been predetermined by her mother and the church. Xiomara has a passion for words and finds an outlet in her school's slam poetry club. Her twin brother and her leather notebook hold all of her secrets, including a new love interest at school. When Mami finds the notebook, she tries to silence Xio's dreams, but Xiomara has more to say.

At the end of *The Poet X*, Xiomara uses a contrapuntal poem in her slam performance. Contrapuntal poems are believed to be influenced by the world of music. "Contrapuntal music is composed of multiple melodies that are relatively independent that are sounded together. In the poetic world, contrapuntal poems are poems that intertwine two (or more) separate poems into a single composition—often by offering one line of poem A and before a corresponding line in poem B from start to finish" (Brewer 2017). The two counterpoints, in music or in writing, then blend together. As the author describes at the end of the audio version of the book, "It's a contrapuntal, which means you can read it from left to right, or you can read it from one stanza down into the next stanza. It's really almost like a 'choose your own adventure' for the reader. They can have whatever experience they want with this poem" (Acevedo 2018).

Contrapuntal Poetry-Writing Activity

To organize thoughts before writing a contrapuntal, ask students to draw a simple T-chart on a blank sheet of paper. Next, have them label the columns "Point" and "Counterpoint." It should look something like this:

Point	Counterpoint

Stick with just a few lines on each side for beginners. As students' proficiency and interest increase, add in as many lines as they need. Each line needs to have at least a few words that can be perceived as an individual thought. Full sentences are fine to use, but they are not necessary. Provide or solicit examples of point and counterpoint to get students going. Start with a practice of something simple, like "Rain is better" versus "Sunshine is better." For this first practice run, have students group in twos or threes to work on completing the T-chart together. After they have had some time to write, ask for volunteers to share reading aloud in a "choose your own adventure" style. First try moving downward, from one stanza to the next, then try reading left to right. Discuss how the methods are similar/different and how the mood of the poem may change. From here, move on to individual contrapuntal writing on a topic of each person's own choosing, expanding length with progress.

Curriculum Connections

CCSS.ELA-LITERACY.CCRA.R.4 CCSS.ELA-LITERACY.CCRA.R.6 CCSS.ELA-LITERACY.CCRA.R.7
CCSS.ELA LITERACY.CCRA.W.2 CCSS.ELA-LITERACY.CCRA.W.3 CCSS.ELA-LITERACY.CCRA.W.4
AASL I.B.3. AASL II.D.2
AASL III.A.2 AASL IV.B4
AASL IV.D.2 AASL V.B.1
AASL VI. C.2

Scan this QR code for an example of the passion and intensity that Acevedo brings to her slam performance, *Hair* (Poetry Slam Inc. 2016). https://www.youtube.com/watch?v=J-DrDINervE

Spoken Word Versus Slam Poetry

Many people use the terms "spoken word poetry" and "slam poetry" interchangeably. Spoken

word poetry is actually a broader category that includes rap, slam poetry, and even stand-up comedy. Think about it this way: hip-hop includes rap, break dancing, deejaying, and graffiti. All rap is hip-hop, but not all hip-hop is rap. Similarly, all slam poetry is spoken word poetry, but not all spoken word poetry is slam poetry. Like Xiomara, the main character of *The Poet X*, author Elizabeth Acevedo performs slam poetry and is a National Poetry Slam champion.

Slam Poetry-Writing Activity

Spoken word poetry is first written on a page and later performed for an audience. Wordplay, slang, rhythm, rhymes, and improvisation are key, as this type of poetry is meant to be performed out loud. Using your senses will help provide imagery that is vivid in the minds of your audience. Include things like sounds, movements, and other sensations, so that your words can be projected into the schema of your listeners. PowerPoetry.org suggests the following:

- *Choose a subject and have attitude.* No attitude, no poem! Feelings and opinions give poetry its "richness." Each poet has a unique perspective and view of the world that no one else has. It is important that a spoken word poem embodies the courage necessary to share oneself with the rest of the world. The key here is to build confidence. We must acknowledge ourselves as writers and understand what we have to say is important. Practice. Practice. Practice.

- *Pick your poetic devices.* Poems that get attention are ones that incorporate simple but powerful poetic elements. Repetition is a device that can help a writer generate exciting poems by just repeating a key phrase or image. Rhyming can enrich your diction and performance. Check out other poetic devices while you're at it. See the Glossary of Poetic Devices in the back of this book.

- *Performance.* Spoken word poems are written to be performed. After your poem is written, practice performing it with the elements of good stage presence in mind. It is important to maintain eye contact—don't stare at the floor or hide behind a piece of paper or your phone. From time to time, look into the eyes of people in the audience to capture their attention. Projection is also crucial, so remember to speak loudly and clearly so that your voice can be heard from a distance. Enunciation helps the listeners to hear exactly what you say. Don't mumble. Speak clearly and distinctly so that the audience can understand what you are saying. Facial expressions help animate your poem. You're not a statue—smile if you're reading something happy, and look angry if your poem is about anger. This might sound silly, but using the appropriate facial expressions help express various emotions in your performance. Gestures such as hand motions and body movements emphasize different elements of your performance. Choose the right gestures for your poem.

- *Memorization.* Once you've memorized your spoken word piece, you can devote more time to your performance. Memorization allows you to be truly in touch with the meaning and the emotional content of your poem, so even if you forget a word or a line, you can improvise (freestyle), which is one of the most important elements of spoken word poetry.

> (Shared with permission from Wiener and PowerPoetry.org, 2019)

Curriculum Connections

CCSS.ELA-LITERACY.CCRA.R.4 CCSS.ELA-LITERACY.CCRA.R.5 CCSS.ELA-LITERACY.CCRA.R.6
CCSS.ELA-LITERACY.CCRA.R.7 CCSS.ELA-LITERACY.CCRA.R.8 CCSS.ELA-LITERACY.CCRA.W.1
CCSS.ELA-LITERACY.CCRA.W.2 CCSS.ELA-LITERACY. CCRA.W.3 CCSS.ELA-LITERACY.CCRA.W.4
CCSS.ELA-LITERACY.CCRA.W.5 AASL.I.B.3 AASL I.C.4 AASL. II.B.1 AASL II.C.2 AASL. II.D.2
AASL.III.D.1. AASL.IV.D.2 AASL.V.B.1 AASL.VI.C.2

Poetry Slam Activity Information

Practicing in small groups is helpful, as students need to feel comfortable performing in front of a group of people. Eventually, after much practice at both writing and performing the poems, a slam can be held. It can be during a class, in front of the entire school, in front of a community organization, and other settings. Many times, community centers, public libraries, and coffee shops host open mic nights where slam poets are featured.

Parameters need to be set for the competition. First, you will need to find some judges. They do not have to be poets, just willing audience members prepared to rate each performance on a 1–10 scale. To prevent ties, have an odd number of judges, like three or five. Teens read their poems without the aid of any costumes, props, or music.

The written poem and the performance of it must be original work. Each poet has a time limit (usually 3 minutes) to perform. Teens should be sure to practice while timing themselves, as going more than 10 seconds overtime results in losing points. Poems should be relatable to the audience; remember to utilize the power of imagery. Practicing with family and friends before the big event will help with timing, nerves, and a smoother delivery. Ask for feedback after practice performances so you can be sure that your poem is conveying a clear message.

Rhythm is of utmost importance and should help carry the moods of the poem with passion and intensity.

Finally, try watching videos of other slam poets on YouTube or Power Poetry.org to model some techniques and give you inspiration. Good luck!

Booked by Kwame Alexander
HMH Books for Young Readers
April 5, 2016
ISBN: 978-0544570986

Grades: 5–8

Content Tags:
Black, books, bullying, crush, divorce, family dynamics, hospitals, library, smart, soccer, sports, surgery, teachers

Summary

Twelve-year-old Nick is a star of the soccer team, and he hates when his dad makes him read the dictionary. In the midst of crushing on April and being bullied by a pair of twins at school, his home life is changing, too. When his mom moves out and there is a health crisis, Nick feels like his world has turned upside down. With the help of vocabulary that he is learning in the dictionary that he had at first resented, as well as a school librarian who hands him inspiring books, Nick finds power through words to help him cope.

Nick uses blackout poetry several times to express himself. Sometimes poets may have trouble coming up with words themselves. Blackout poetry is a great way to remove that writer's block, by basically making a redacted version of a page, with the words that are not blacked out creating a poem of their own. See pages 51, 78, and 284 of the book for examples of Nick's blackout poems.

Blackout Poetry Activity

Using discarded library books or old newspapers, have teens select a page to use. Next, advise them to scan the page, looking for anchor words—words that have strong or multiple meanings that can serve as the core of the poem. Using a pencil, lightly circle words that stand out as possibly being connected to the anchor words. After circling at least 10–15 words, list them in order on a sheet of paper. Read through the list and begin to piece the words together to create the lines of a poem. You may find that you need to discard certain words that don't seem to make sense together. You can also eliminate parts of words if doing so helps to keep or clarify the meaning of the poem. This is common with word endings. If you find that you are missing a word or an article (such as "a," "an," or "the"), or need more words to help the poem make sense, go back into the original poem text, and it just might be there. Also remember to remove the circles from any words in the original text that have been discarded.

Sharpie markers work best to truly black out the words. At first, use just black to make a redacted page look like the ones in *Booked*. After some practice, try using different colors to obscure the words and create an illustration on the page that complements the poem or directs the reader on a particular path, such as in Figure 2.1.

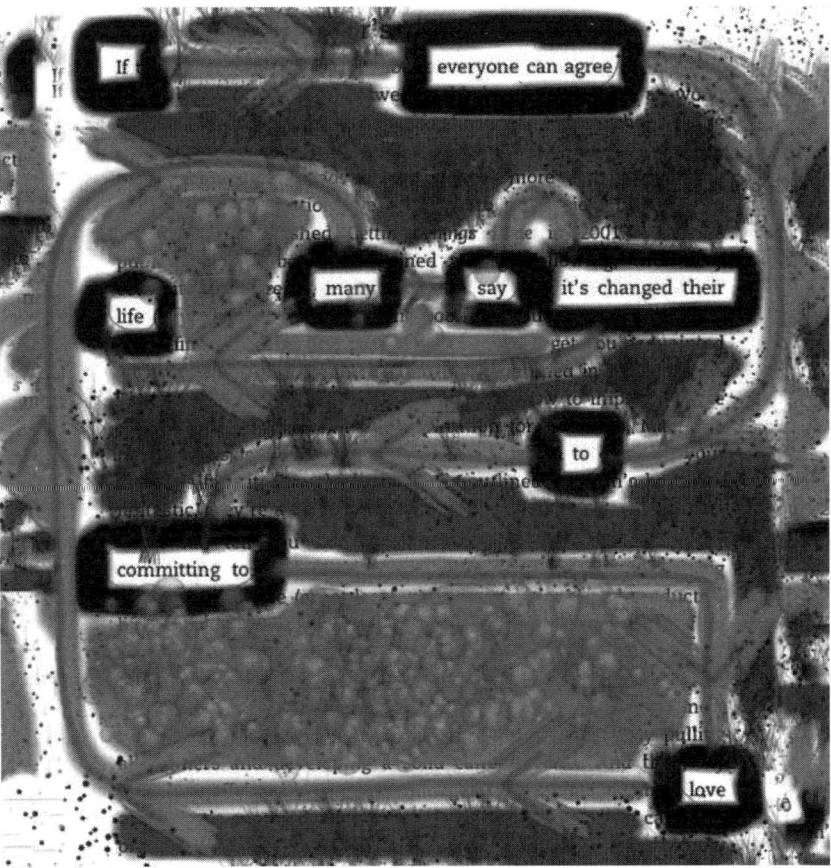

Figure 2.1 Blackout poetry sample.

Curriculum Connections

CCSS.ELA-LITERACY.CCRA.R.2 CCSS.ELA-LITERACY.CCRA.R.4
CCSS.ELA-LITERACY.CCRA.R.5
CCSS.ELA-LITERACY.CCRA.R.7 CCSS.ELA-LITERACY.CCRA.W.2
CCSS.ELA-LITERACY.CCRA.W.4
AASL.I.B.3 AASL II.D.2 AASL.IV.A.3 AASL.V.B.2

Acrostic Poetry Activity

Nick's dad has him read the entire dictionary to improve his vocabulary, an activity that he complains about throughout the book. This activity will involve making an acrostic poem using the dictionary. The most simple and commonly used form of an acrostic poem is where the first letters of the lines spell out a word or phrase. It might look something like this:

D ear

O ld

G us

S nores

For more challenge, try longer words or more complex acrostics, such as last letter instead of first letter, or first- *and* last-letter acrostic poems, which are called "double acrostics." Ask teens to write the word "DICTIONARY" vertically on a blank sheet of paper. Next, students come up with a word that begins with each letter in "DICTIONARY" to create an acrostic poem that brings to mind how they feel about dictionaries or how the words relate to a dictionary. Invite teens to share when finished. To extend the activity, ask students to come up with their own words from *Booked* to make more acrostic creations. Examples might be "soccer," "April," and "appendix."

Curriculum Connections

CCSS.ELA-LITERACY.CCRA.R.2 CCSS.ELA-LITERACY.CCRA.R.4
CCSS.ELA-LITERACY.CCRA.R.5
CCSS.ELA-LITERACY.CCRA.R.7 CCSS.ELA-LITERACY.CCRA.W.3
CCSS.ELA-LITERACY.CCRA.W.4
AASL.I.A.2 AASL.I.B.3 AASL II.D.2 AASL.IV.A.3 AASL.V.B.2

The Crossover by Kwame Alexander
HMH Books for Young Readers
March 18, 2014
ISBN: 978-0544107717

Grades: 6 and up

Content Tags:
basketball, Black, death, family dynamics, humor, sports, twins

Summary

Twins Josh and Jordan Bell have mad skills on the basketball court, which they inherited from their legendary father, Charles "Chuck" Bell. Life is more than basketball, though, as the story of their family plays out through brisk, rhythmic verse that culminates both on and off the court, with game-changing consequences.

March Madness: Poetry Edition

Josh and Jordan might be battling it out on the court, but we can have some fun with poetry using typical tournament brackets, such as used during the NCAA Men's Basketball Championships (aka "March Madness"). Let the students select their favorite poems written by other authors, and then mark each entry onto the blank bracket (for whole-group purposes, a large whiteboard works great). Battling in pairs, students read their poems aloud to the class. Then the class votes, and the winning poem advances to the next round. The process continues until the Final Four, the finalists, and the eventual winner are selected. This can be repeated for another set of known poems or, for more of a challenge, the students can write their own poems and duel it out using the same process. Because this is open-ended, with a blank bracket, it can be used many times in many ways.

See an example of a blank bracket in Figure 2.2.

Curriculum Connections

CCSS.ELA-LITERACY.CCRA.R.5 CCSS.ELA-LITERACY.CCRA.R.7
CCSS.ELA-LITERACY.CCRA.R.9
CCSS.ELA-LITERACY.CCRA.W.9 AASL.I.A.2 AASL.I.C.1 AASL.
II.B.1. AASL.II.C.2 AASL.III .D.1
AASL.IV.A.1. AASL.IV.A.2. AASL.IV.A.3 AASL.IV.C.3 AASL.V.A.3
AASL VI.A.3

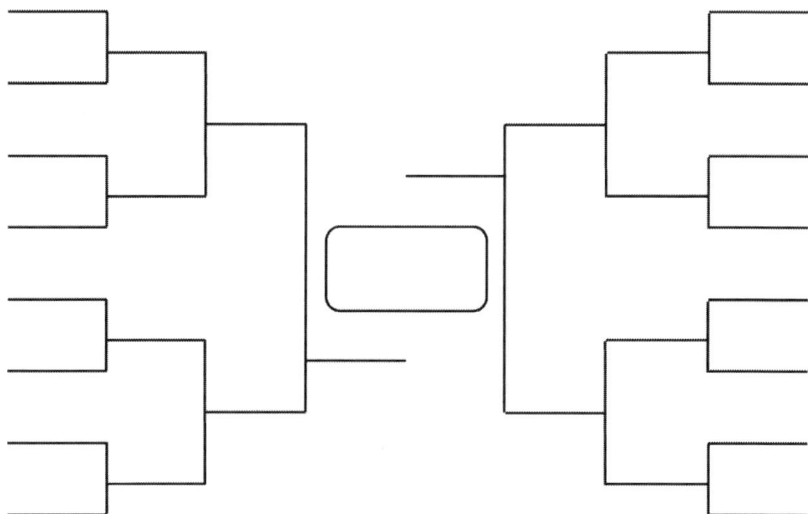

Figure 2.2 March Madness poetry bracket.

***Rebound* by Kwame Alexander**
HMH Books for Young Readers
April 2, 2018
ISBN: 978-0544868137

Grades: 6 and up

Content Tags:
arcade games, basketball, Black, comics, death, intergenerational, jazz, overcoming fears, sports

Summary

In this prequel to *The Crossover,* readers explore the background of Josh and Jordan Bell's illustrious father, Charlie "Chuck" Bell. When Chuck spends a summer at his grandparents' home, it turns out that he and the twins have much more in common than basketball alone . . . and Filthy McNasty.

Because this is a prequel to *The Crossover,* the two books *could* be read as stand-alone stories, or in either order. However, reading *The Crossover* first lends itself to more discovery later of the family background and allows readers to recognize familiar character names.

Comics Poetry Activity

Chuck Bell's narrative is presented both in verse and in comic panels throughout this book. Some may wonder what comics are doing in the middle of a verse novel. Here is some good information on how they are related:

> Comics, like poetry, concentrate on the aesthetic audio-visual arrangement of segments whereas other literary forms are more concerned with syntax than spatial composition. In addition to their concentration on formal qualities, comics and poetry both incorporate meter, juxtaposition, line breaks, enjambment, countermeasure and disjunctive strategies, amongst other typographic and aesthetic devices. In both comics and poetry, visual and verbal components can be repeated, layered, removed from panels or presented as a simultaneous series of moments not bound by linear grid lines or narrative closure. (McCloud 20 via Bennett 2014)
>
> Heightened language—one possible or partial definition of poetry—isn't the first thing one associates with comics. Yet comic book artists take into account the way words appear on the page to a degree poets will find familiar. How many lines should accompany each image? How high should the dialogue balloon float? The ratio of printed words to blank space plays a role in whether a poem or strip succeeds. The best of the daily humor strips (think *Peanuts*) have produced thousands of word-and-picture episodes that occupy about the same thought-space as a good short poem; the terseness can resemble haiku. (Brown 2007)

There are many blank comic panels available to download online. Figure 2.3 shows an example of one from https://medialoot.com/blog/free-printable -comic-strip-templates (Sanchez 2018). These give teens an opportunity to try their hand at comic poetry. They can do them individually as pages, or they can work in small groups to create a book.

Curriculum Connections

CCSS.ELA-LITERACY.CCRA.R.7 CCSS.ELA-LITERACY.CCRA.W.2
CCSS.ELA-LITERACY.CCRA.W.3
CCSS.ELA-LITERACY.CCRA.W.4 CCSS.ELA-LITERACY.
CCRA.W.6 AASL.I.B.3 AASL.II.C.2
AASL.III.A.1 AASL IV.B.4 AASL V. B.1 AASL.VI.C.2

Figure 2.3 Medialoot.com comic strip template.

***Solo* by Kwame Alexander**
Blink
August 1, 2017
ISBN: 978-0310761839

Grades: 8 and up

Content Tags:
addiction, adoption, alcoholism, Black, death, family dynamics, family secrets, first love/sex, musicians

Summary

Born into rock star royalty, Blade clings to his girlfriend, Chapel, in the absence of his deceased mother and his addicted, unreliable father, Rutherford.

When Blade is humiliated by Rutherford drunkenly crashing into his high school graduation speech, he loses Chapel and much of his hope. When a hidden family secret is unearthed, Blade travels to Ghana to unravel his own history and attempt to rebuild his life.

Clerihew Activity

Rutherford certainly got on Blade's nerves pretty regularly. Writing a clerihew would have likely been a good way for him to vent.

Is there a celebrity or other famous person who really gets on your nerves? Have you ever wished that you could tell someone what exactly it is that bugs you? Well, now you can join some other poets by writing a clerihew—the best way to (poetically) insult someone.

Mr. Clerihew, who are you? Edmund Clerihew Bentley, a twentieth-century humorist and novelist, invented the clerihew form. He wanted to make fun of certain famous people, and he decided that there's no better way to do so than with poetry—and with laughs!

This is a biography that's actually fun to read—because you get to write it. Clerihews are essentially short, humorous biographies about people who are well known, like celebrities or historical figures. Starting with their full name, you pick the subject and information about them that you'd like to include in the poem. Their name is either solely the first line of the poem, or within the first line. After that, there are only three more lines to go.

Time to rhyme! Clerihews follow an *AABB* rhyme scheme, which means that the first and second lines should rhyme with one another, and so should the third and fourth lines. For this type of poem, there are no rules about line length because it is more successful when it has a bouncy, yet jagged vibe.

Not a lie, just an exaggeration. The trick to writing a clerihew is to include facts about the subject, but to arrange them in a way that makes the poem comical. One way to do this is to take two events that occurred far apart from one another and write about them as if they took place one right after the other. For example, "She gave him life / He got a wife" are two lines with statements that may be true about a person, but they didn't happen that quickly.

Time to vent! One of the reasons why the clerihew is such a fun type of poem to read and write is because they're so short—a lot like knock-knock jokes—and they make fun of people everyone knows. Take a stab at writing one, or a whole collection!

(Shared with permission from Wiener and PowerPoetry.org, 2019)

Curriculum Connections

CCSS.ELA-LITERACY.CCRA.R.3 f CCSS.ELA-LITERACY.
CCRA.R.4 CCSS.ELA-LITERACY.CCRA.R.8

CCSS.ELA-LITERACY.CCRA.W.2 CCSS.ELA-LITERACY.
CCRA.W.3 CCSS.ELA-LITERACY.CCRA.W.4
AASL.I.A.2 AASL.I.B.3 AASL.II.C.2 AASL.IV.B.4 AASL.IV.D.2
AASL V. B.2 AASL.VI.C.2

Shout by Laurie Halse Anderson
Viking Books for Young Readers
March 12, 2019
ISBN: 978-0670012107

Grades: 9 and up

Content Tags:
consent, empowerment, #MeToo, molestation, sex, sexual
assault/abuse

Summary

Twenty years after her haunting novel *Speak* was published, Laurie Halse
Anderson follows up with this vulnerable, compelling memoir in verse that
advocates for those suffering from sexual assault. The demand for consent is
explicit and is both an acknowledgment and rallying cry for survivors. Raw,
spirited, and timeless, readers are urged to not just speak, but to SHOUT their
voices loud and clear.

Heal Your Heart Poetry Activity

Some terms tied to the book *Shout* are shout, consent, and empowerment. Teens select one of these terms as anchors for their own poetry. Visual
poetry styles are suggested to enhance the urgency and importance of the
words. Haiku, concrete, acrostic,
diamante, and sonnet are some style
options. As always, remember that
the thesaurus is your friend to help
find alternative words to fit your
poetry.

Laurie Halse Anderson has learned
that writing can help heal your heart.
Scan the QR code to hear her
comments (Penguin Random House
Audio 2019). https://www.youtube
.com/watch?v=ttzJR5tGTTA.

Haiku are short poems that don't
rhyme, but instead focus on the
total number of syllables in each
line. Traditional haiku use a total of
17 syllables spread over three lines
of text. Most haiku use a formula
of 5-7-5: The first and third lines

contain 5 syllables, and the middle line contains 7 (Wiener and PowerPoetry .org 2019).

Concrete poetry, also called "visual" or "shape" poetry, was created as a way to combine image and poetry. The importance of language is emphasized in this type of art, as the shapes the words make are just as important as what they say (Wiener and PowerPoetry.org 2019).

The most simple and commonly used form of an acrostic poem is where the first letters of each line spell out the word or phrase. They begin something like this:

S

H

O

U

T

The writer then adds words starting with each letter that connect with what the anchor term means to them.

A diamante is a poem of seven lines that does not rhyme. The first and last lines are the shortest, while the lines in the middle are longer, and the lines are also centered, which gives diamante poems a diamond shape. Because *diamante* is the Italian word for *diamond*, these poems are named for their rhombus shape.

Kenn Nesbitt (2011) advises the following rules for diamantes:

Diamantes are seven lines long.

The first and last lines have just one word.

The second and sixth lines have two words.

The third and fifth lines have three words.

And the fourth line has four words.

Lines 1, 4, and 7 have nouns.

Lines 2 and 6 have adjectives.

Lines 3 and 5 have verbs.

Here's an easy way to visualize all three rules:

Noun
Adj., Adj.
Verb, Verb, Verb
Noun, Noun, Noun, Noun
Verb, Verb, Verb
Adj., Adj.
Noun

There are two types of these poems: synonym and antonym diamantes. In a synonym diamante, the nouns in the first and last lines means basically the same thing. In an antonym diamante, the nouns in the first and last lines are opposites. Also, centering your poem in the middle of the page helps make the diamond shape more apparent.

A sonnet can be a perfect style of poetry for expressing strong emotions. There are varied types of sonnets, so for this activity, use the following format. Sonnets are 14-line poems with a variable rhyme scheme. There must be three sets of 4 lines, followed by one set of 2 lines. The sets of 4 lines are called "quatrains," and the last set of 2 lines is a "couplet." The rhyme scheme is as follows:

First quatrain: *ABAB*

Second quatrain: *CDCD*

Third quatrain: *EFEF*

Couplet: *GG*

As always, teens have the right to privacy and are not required to share their poems about sensitive topics. Those who want to write more can certainly do so in a poetry journal. Volunteers may share if they wish.

Curriculum Connections

CCSS.ELA-LITERACY.CCRA.R.2 CCSS.ELA-LITERACY.CCRA.R.4
CCSS.ELA-LITERACY.CCRA.R.6
CCSS.ELA-LITERACY.CCRA.R.7 CCSS.ELA-LITERACY.CCRA.W.1
CCSS.ELA-LITERACY.CCRA.W.2
CCSS.ELA-LITERACY.CCRA.W.4 AASL.I.A.2 AASL.I.B.3 AASL.
II.A.2 AASL.IV.B.4 AASL.V.B.1
AASL.VI.C.2

Reader Resources for Sexual Violence

- RAINN (which stands for "Rape, Abuse, & Incest National Network") is the largest antisexual violence organization in the United States. In partnership with more than 1,000 local sexual assault service providers, it operates the National Sexual Assault Hotline [800-656-HOPE (4673)]. Visit RAINN.org or RAINN.org/es (en español).
- End Rape on Campus works to end campus sexual violence by supporting survivors, education, and policy reform. Visit endrapeoncampus.org.
- FORGE is a national transgender antiviolence organization that helps transgender, gender nonconforming, and gender nonbinary survivors of sexual assault. Visit forge-forward.org.

- IGNITE supports survivors of sexual violence and domestic violence who are Deaf, DeafBlind, or Hard of Hearing. Visit deafignite.org.

- 1IN6 supports male victims of unwanted sexual experience, sexual abuse, and sexual violence. Visit 1in6.org.

- National Sexual Violence Resource Center is a national information and resource organization that works with the Centers for Disease Control and Prevention to collect and share resources with people and organizations working to understand and eliminate sexual violence. Visit nsvrc.org.

Reader Resources for Mental Health

- To Write Love on Her Arms works to help people who are struggling with depression, addiction, self-injury, and suicide find help and hope. Visit twloha .com.

- Suicide Prevention Lifeline is a national network of crisis centers that offer free emotional support 24/7, including specific resources for kids, LGBTQ+ people, Native Americans, Deaf and Hard of Hearing people, loss survivors, attempt survivors, disaster survivors, and veterans. Visit suicideprevention lifeline.org or call 800-273-TALK (8255).

- The Trevor Project provides crisis intervention and suicide prevention for LGBTQ+ youth, offering a hotline (phone, text, ad online chat), and educational resources for family and allies. Visit thetrevorproject.org.

- Safe Horizon offers resources to survivors of domestic violence, human trafficking, child abuse, stalking, and youth homelessness. Visit safehorizon.org.

- The Substance Abuse and Mental Healtlh Services Administration is an agency in the U.S. Department of Health and Human Services that provides services for people struggling with mental health and substance abuse issues. Visit samhsa.gov.

They Call Me Güero: A Border Kid's Poems
by David Bowles
Artwork by Zeke Peña
Cinco Puntos Press
November 27, 2018
ISBN: 978-1947627062

Grades: 5–8

Content Tags:
bookworm, bullying, Chicano, death of a pet, Dominican, family dynamics, intergenerational, Korean, Latinx, Mexican American, Nuhuatl, Quinceañera

Summary

Güero is a pale-skinned boy living on the border with his loving Mexican American family. He is wise beyond his years, wondering things like: if he is Catholic and his friends are Mormon and Christian, how can everyone be right? After the death of his dog, his sister's quinceañera provides the family with a bright ray of sunshine. Güero's teacher buoys his writing, telling him, "Poetry is the clearest lens for viewing the world." Together with his Bookworm Squad friends, Los Bobbys, he manages a bottle rocket fiasco and attempts to get the girl that he is crushing on hard. When he encounters the school bully, help comes from an unexpected place. A glossary in the back of the book provides information about Spanish terms and phrases.

Couplet Poetry Activity

Güero uses couplets to describe his days in the poem "Sundays" on page 38. A couplet is two lines of verse, placed together, that are linked by both rhythm and rhyme. The quick pacing and concise language of couplets are used by poets to make their poems grab the reader's attention. It is considered closed when the two lines form a bound unit of grammar, such as a sentence.

Have teens choose a day of the week to write about. First, they brainstorm a list of rhyming pairs that come to mind about their day of choice. Next, they sequence the pairs and write couplets. Some may be closed, while others may continue to the next stanza of lines. Remind students to use a thesaurus for help finding synonyms and antonyms to fit their rhymes.

Curriculum Connections

> CCSS.ELA-LITERACY.CCRA.R.4 CCSS.ELA-LITERACY.CCRA.R.5
>   CCSS.ELA-LITERACY.CCRA.W.3
> CCSS.ELA-LITERACY.CCRA.W.4 AASL.I.B.3 AASL.II.C.2 AASL.
>   IV.B.4 AASL.V.B.1 AASL.VI.C.2

Rondeau Poetry Activity

When Güero's teacher assigns a unit about masks, he is intrigued.

> To me, the best thing is that
> masks can either hide or reveal your identity.
> You can pretend to be something else—
> a god, a monster, a princess, a priest—
> or you can show your true self,

your animal soul,
your skeleton.
(Bowles 2018, 35)

This passage brings to mind the well-known poem by Paul Laurence Dunbar, "We Wear the Mask" (1896).

We wear the mask that grins and lies,
It hides our cheeks and shades our eyes,—
This debt we pay to human guile;
With torn and bleeding hearts we smile
And mouth with myriad subtleties,

Why should the world be over-wise,
In counting all our tears and sighs?
Nay, let them only see us, while
We wear the mask.

We smile, but oh great Christ, our cries
To thee from tortured souls arise.
We sing, but oh the clay is vile
Beneath our feet, and long the mile,
But let the world dream otherwise,
We wear the mask!

Note: This poem is in the public domain.

The metaphors abound regarding masks in the works of both Bowles and Dunbar. Although Dunbar originally wrote this poem for oppressed Black people, I believe that today, it also applies to Black Indigenous People of Color (BIPOC) people of all kinds that are currently being oppressed, including Mexicans at the border, Muslims, Native American/Indigenous, LGBTQ+ people, and others.

The form of Dunbar's poem is rondeau, in iambic tetrameter. To put it simply, a rondeau is a type of poem that runs between 10 and 15 lines in length and is organized into three stanzas. The opening words, "We wear the mask," become the refrain of the poem, which repeats at the end of the second and third stanzas.

"It has only two rhymes, which look something like this in terms of patterns: AABBA AABc AABAc, where A and B represent a particular end rhyme (line 1 rhymes with lines 2 and 5; line 3 rhymes with line 4, etc.), and c here represents the refrain" (Schmoop Editorial Team, 2008).

Sound confusing? The rondeau is actually one of the simpler types of verse because it only has those two rhymes. Once those are all set, you just need to keep track of where they occur. For example, in Dunbar's poem, the first set of rhymes (A) consists of the words "lies," "eyes," "subtleties" (which rhymes visually rather than aurally), "wise," "sighs," "cries," "arise," and "otherwise." The next set (B) consists of the words "guile," "smile," "while," "vile," and "mile." Finally the refrain stands alone, without a rhyme.

So why do poets go with specific forms like this? Usually, it is the case that the words and themes can be accented in a lyrical sort of way. Think about how when you listen to a song, you can anticipate when the chorus will occur. This is comparable to the refrains and the rondeau.

That wraps up the rondeau. Next is the meter. Iambic tetrameter is one of the most commonly used rhythms in poetry. It is composed of unstressed, then stressed syllable pairs (iambs) occurring four times ("tetra" = four). The beat sounds something like daDum daDum daDUM daDUM. For example, hear it here:

We wear the mask that grins and lies
U   S   U   S   U   S   U   S

Bingo—that's iambic tetrameter. Typically, the only diversion occurring in a rondeau is during the refrain, where we get a total of only four syllables instead of eight in this case. So in *We Wear the Mask,* the only lines that are not in iambic tetrameter are the refrains at the end of the second and third stanzas. The rhythm of this meter also lends itself often to songs (Schmoop 2008).

Remind teens that as Güero stated, people wear masks to hide or to reveal their true identities. As teens begin to write their own rondeaus, they can choose whichever type of mask they prefer to write about.

Curriculum Connections

CCSS.ELA-LITERACY.CCRA.R.1 CCSS.ELA-LITERACY.CCRA.R.2
    CCSS.ELA-LITERACY.CCRA.R.4
CCSS.ELA-LITERACY.CCRA.R.6 CCSS.ELA-LITERACY.CCRA.R.9
    CCSS.ELA-LITERACY.CCRA.W.3
CCSS.ELA-LITERACY.CCRA.W.4 AASL.I.A.2 AASL.I.B.3
    AASL.I.D.3 AASL.II.B.3 AASL.IV.B.2
AASL.IV.C.2 AASL.IV.D.2 AASL.V.B.1 AASL.VI.C.2

Freakboy **by Kristin Elizabeth Clark**
Farrar, Straus and Giroux BFYR
October 22, 2013
ISBN: 978-0374324728

Grades: 7 and up

Content Tags:
domestic violence, first love/sex, foster care, gender fluidity, gender identity, prostitution, self-acceptance, suicidal ideation, therapy, transgender, transphobia, wrestling

Summary

Freakboy is the story of three characters whose lives weave together. Brendan is a wrestler with a beautiful girlfriend, Vanessa. Only Brendan doesn't want to just date her, he wants to *be* her. For her part, Vanessa wonders why he is pulling away. Angel, a trans girl who grew up in foster care, guides Brendan as he examines his own gender identity questioning. Brendan's mother encourages him to find a new therapist, which he does "not to cure . . . just to help figure out." Please note that this book was written by a cisgender woman, and it represents a trans story, but not *all* trans stories.

Concrete Poetry Activity

Poetry itself is a type of art, but did you know that you can create poetry to look like art, too? By paying close attention to the way that you write or type the actual words, you can create an image that connects to the story your poem tells! Here are some tips to get started.

The author of *Freakboy* uses concrete poetry in several places throughout the book. Creatively arranging the placement of words can propel them into more intense meanings. For example, on page 186 of the book, the word "exploded" is repeated and positioned to form an explosion that translated into fireworks. Another example of concrete poetry is a verse shaped like a bowling pin on page 162, which accentuates the setting.

Purpose: Concrete poetry, also called "visual" or "shape" poetry, was created as a way to combine image and poetry. The importance of language is emphasized in this type of art, as the shapes the words make are just as important as what they say.

Write: With concrete poetry, it's a good idea to first write out your whole poem without putting it into a shape. There are no rules when it comes to a concrete poem, so you're free to let your imagination run wild and create any story you like! Don't worry about the length of your poem, but remember that the more words you have, the bigger your shape will be.

Shape: Pick a shape that you want your poem to create. If someone looks at your poem from far away, they will see the outline of the shape, but up close, they will actually be able to read the words. Knowing this, you will probably want to pick a pretty simple shape. First, think of what story your poem will tell, and then match the shape to the theme of the poem. For example, if you are writing a love poem, you might want the poem to be shaped like a heart.

Draw: You don't need to be an artist to make this poem look great! Just draw an outline of the shape you picked, either on paper or with a drawing tool from a computer program like Paint (or Photoshop if you're feeling fancy). If you're going to draw your concrete poem by hand, you can always scan the picture and upload it to your computer so you have a virtual version too!

Words: Remember that with a concrete poem, the words are just as important as the shapes they make. So it's a good idea to experiment with using bold, italics, or even colors to add shade and texture to the words or to make whatever shape you use look three-dimensional! Then, either by hand or using a software program, paste the words of the poem that you've written onto the outline of the shape in the order that you want them to be read! Now, you will have created your own original poetic picture!

Make a Scene: Don't just stop at one shape—make a whole scene! Go crazy and write a whole bunch of poems that are different lengths and turn them into all different sizes and shapes to create an image that tells its own story.

(Shared with permission from Wiener and PowerPoetry.org, 2019)

Curriculum Connections

CCSS.ELA-LITERACY.CCRA.R.2 CCSS.ELA-LITERACY.CCRA.R.4
    CCSS.ELA-LITERACY.CCRA.R.6
CCSS.ELA-LITERACY.CCRA.W.1 CCSS.ELA-LITERACY.
    CCRA.W.2 CCSS.ELA-LITERACY.CCRA.W.4
AASL.I.B.2 AASL.II.D.2 AASL.III.C.2 AASL.IV.B.4 AASL.V.B.1
    AASL.VI.C.2

A FEW IMPORTANT TIPS FOR ENGAGING WITH TRANSGENDER TEENS

Respect the names and pronouns transgender youth have chosen for themselves. If you don't know—ask. Model that respect in front of all students and colleagues.

The experiences of LGBT youth vary greatly. Lumping LGBT experiences together is a mistake. For example, transgender and gender-nonconforming youth often face more hostility and bullying at school than their lesbian, gay and bisexual peers.

Supportive school staff can make all the difference. One educator can make a difference—but the goal is building an inclusive and welcoming school.

All students have the right to use the bathroom that corresponds to their gender identity. A transgender student should never be forced to use alternative facilities to make other students comfortable.

Mentorship is instrumental for trans students' success. When possible, seek out or establish a trans-to-trans mentorship program for students. Adult mentors can serve as a crucial support system for trans students and provide models for what it looks like to live life as a transgender person.

Curriculum and instruction play a big part in supporting trans youth. Including transgender figures and narratives in the curriculum helps ensure that trans students do not feel alone. Paying attention to and affirming non-gender-binary identities in student work is also very important.

Always trust and defer to transgender youth. If you are a non-trans-identified adult, don't question what your trans student is going through. Follow their lead and provide your continued support along the way.

Be aware of bias—your own and others'. Uncover any transphobia and personal bias you may hold. Learn to recognize and interrupt gender-identity-based bullying and harassment.

(Reprinted with permission of Teaching Tolerance, a project of the Southern Poverty Law Center. https://www.tolerance.org/magazine/tell-transgender-students-were-still-here-for-you, 2019.)

Resources from Clark

Trevor Lifeline
866-488-7386 or visit www.thetrevorproject.org
Provides crisis intervention to LGBTQ+ youth

CenterLink, an international database of LTBTQ+ centers
www.lgbtcenters.org/Centers/find-a-center.aspx

TransYouth Family Allies, Inc.
www.imatyfa.org
Assists families with trans and gender-varied youth

You Remind Me of You: A Poetry Memoir
by Eireann Corrigan
PUSH
February 1, 2002
ISBN: 978-0439297714

Grades: 8 and up

Content Tags:
body image, Christian, drugs, eating disorders, first love/sex, interfaith dating, Jewish, mental illness, recovery, self-harm, suicide, therapy

Summary

This memoir in verse details Eireann Corrigan's journey in and out of treatment facilities for eating disorders, as well as her proximity to dying. When her boyfriend attempts suicide, her path to recovery changes. The formatting of the book varies from poetry and interviews between herself and her therapist.

Body Image Poetry Activity

Clearly, Corrigan did not have a positive view of her own body, which led to her eating disorder. Cultivating a positive and loving body image is essential to well-being and happiness. It takes a healthy mindset to reach self-acceptance. Many feel pressured to obtain a certain social and/or cultural ideal of beauty, especially given the images depicting "idealized" bodies in the media.

Other pressures can come from the people in your life, like family and friends. They can have a huge impact on how you feel about your own body, either with positive or not-so-positive comments about certain body types (including their own bodies). That said, it is possible to establish a loving relationship with your own body, no matter what shape or size. Here are some actions that you can take to get started (shared with permission from Wiener and PowerPoetry.org 2019):

> **Research.** What or who influences you the most? Are there certain people you talk to or shows you watch that heavily impact how you feel about yourself, positively or negatively? It's common to compare yourself to others you know or admire, including celebrities. Think about how certain people and images impact your life—then you can begin to focus on the people and resources who help you feel positive.

> **Create.** Look for safe spaces where you are free to speak openly and feel comfortable in your own skin. This space should provide healthy messages

about all bodies, regardless of color, shape, size, or anything else. If it is difficult to find this space near you, create it—bring together friends and people you trust to make this a place where others feel comfortable too.

Transform. Learning and practicing to eliminate negative pressures and ideas about how you should look is an important step in creating positive and healthy self-esteem. In order to begin changing the societal pressures and expectations of beauty and perfection, you should think about how you can love your body rather than how you are told to love your body. Focus on finding messages that instill self-love for you.

Think. Everyone has her/his own perspective and idea on what a healthy body is. Everyone is different, and those differences should be celebrated, not criticized. Create an ethic with your body in which you promise to accept and love it unconditionally and ensure your safe space is shared by others in your group.

Get started. Do things that leave you feeling positive and surround your-self with people who love themselves—the people you spend time with impacts the way you see yourself greatly. Write about your feelings towards your body, positive or negative. It's important to share your experiences with others for support. Think about any challenges you face and what tools you or people you know have used to help develop a healthy, positive attitude towards body image.

Curriculum Connections

CCSS.ELA-LITERACY.CCRA.R.4 CCSS.ELA-LITERACY.CCRA.R.6
   CCSS.ELA-LITERACY.CCRA.R.7
CCSS.ELA-LITERACY.CCRA.W.1 CCSS.ELA-LITERACY.
   CCRA.W.2 CCSS.ELA-LITERACY.CCRA.W.3
CCSS.ELA-LITERACY.CCRA.W.4 CCSS.ELA-LITERACY.
   CCRA.W.7 CCSS.ELA-LITERACY.CCRA.W.8
AASL.I.A.2 AASL.I.B.3 AASL.I.D.3 AASL.II.B.2 AASL.III.C.2 AASL.
   IV.A.1 AASL.IV.A.2
AASL.IV.A.3 AASL.IV.B.4 AASL.IV.D.2 AASL.V.A.2 AASL.VI.C.2

Resources for Help with Eating Disorders

NEDA (National Eating Disorders Association)
Call the helpline at 800- 931-2237 or visit www.nationaleatingdisorders.org/.
For crisis situations, text "NEDA" to 741741 to be connected with a trained vol-
   unteer at the Crisis Text Line.

NIMH (National Institute of Mental Health)
www.nimh.nih.gov/health/topics/eating-disorders/index.shtml

Sanctuary Somewhere by Brenna Dimmig
West 44 Books
April 1, 2019
ISBN: 978-1538382837

Grades: 7–12 *[can serve as high interest–low reading level (hi-lo) for older teens]*

Content Tags:
college applications, DACA, ICE, immigrants, meteorology, Mexican, undocumented

Summary

Osmel's world shatters when he finds out that he is undocumented. Seventeen years old and dreaming of becoming a meteorologist, his education and career dreams may now be an impossibility. When ICE begins raiding the orchards where his family works, he wonders if his family will ever feel peaceful and safe in the place they consider home.

Where I'm From Poetry Activity

Osmel grapples with understanding where he is from when he discovers that he is undocumented. However, does our place of birth designate where we are from, or the experiences that have shaped our lives? Former Kentucky poet laureate George Ella Lyon was tired of hatred and xenophobia spreading through our country. She joined forces with Julie Landsman, an educator, writer, and activist, to find a way to help give people a voice through the I Am From Project. With Lyon's poem as a starting point, their goal was to create a network of teachers, librarians, community leaders, writers, and other professionals. This network would then encourage creative "I Am From . . ." works not only in poems, but also through dance, art, song, and drama.

Read "Where I'm From" aloud (Lyon 2015). The full poem can be found at http://www.georgeellalyon.com/where.html.

"You'll notice that it is basically a list of experiences that shaped her into the person she is today. Brainstorm a list of people, places, foods, sports, music, family sayings, etc., that have made you You. Then play with the arrangement of these images till you find one you like. Poems are like jigsaw puzzles made of sound, so reading out loud will help you hear where the pieces fit" (Kentucky Arts Council 2018).

Scan this QR code to hear Lyon reading her poem (1993).

Lyon suggests doing this yourself before leading a group, in order to give you ideas of ways that you may want to adapt the process to suit your group. "You can do this! Everybody makes lists. The key is not to worry about what you put down, what order it comes in, of whether it sounds poem-like to you. Just get words on the page. Or screen. You might do this in short bursts over several days. (That's what I did.) Then get your pages together, underline the lines you like best, and fiddle with the order. Read it out loud to see how it sounds. Check for places you could zoom in; for example, if you wrote "I'm from the first car I drove," you can bring us in closer by adding "a bean-brown '75 Pinto." Above all, have fun. It's your life. It's your writing. You can't go wrong" (Lyons via *I Am From Project,* 2018).

Curriculum Connections

CCSS.ELA-LITERACY.CCRA.R.1 CCSS.ELA-LITERACY.CCRA.R.3
    CCSS.ELA-LITERACY.CCRA.R.4
CCSS.ELA-LITERACY.CCRA.R.5 CCSS.ELA-LITERACY.CCRA.R.6
    CCSS.ELA-LITERACY.CCRA.W.3
CCSS.ELA-LITERACY.CCRA.W.4 CCSS.ELA-LITERACY.
    CCRA.W.8 AASL.I.A.2 AASL.I.D.3
AASL.II.A.2 AASL.II.B.3 AASL. II. D.3 AASL.III.C.2 AASL.IV.B.2
    AASL.V.B.1 AASL.VI.C.2

Resources for Immigrants

ILRC (Immigrant Legal Resource Center)
https://www.ilrc.org/community-resources

Know Your Rights Toolkit
www.ilrc.org/prepare-your-community-assert-their-rights-against-possible-ice
    -arrests

ACLU (American Civil Liberties Union)
www.aclu.org/issues/immigrants-rights

Enchanted Air: Two Cultures, Two Wings:
A Memoir by Margarita Engle
Atheneum Books for Young Readers
August 4, 2015
ISBN: 978-1481435222

Grades: 6–10

Content Tags:
Cold War, Cuban American, Cuban Missile Crisis,
family dynamics, horses, immigrants, Latinx, torn
between cultures/places

Summary

Margarita Engle's memoir in verse describes her life growing up torn
between two cultures during the Cold War. Born of a Cuban mother and an
American father, she doesn't understand how the two countries she loves so
much can hate each other so much. She longs to take a plane through the
Enchanted Air to be a part of both places of her heart.

Communication Poem Activity: "The Visitor"

When Margarita's Abuelita comes from Cuba for a visit, she marvels that
"even though they can't speak the same language, Abuelita and Grandma seem
to understand each other." Reread pages 55–56, and then write a poem in free
verse or a style of choice. The poem should describe how people can find alternative ways to communicate and understand each other, even when they
don't speak the same language.

Curriculum Connections

> CCSS.ELA-LITERACY.CCRA.W.2
> CCSS.ELA-LITERACY.CCRA.W.3
> AASL.I.A.2. AASL.I.B.3 AASL.I.D.3 AASL.II.B.3 AASL.IV.A.1.
>   AASL.IV.A.2 AASL.IV.B.3
> AASL.IV.D.2 AASL.V.D.1 AASL.VI.A.3 AASL.VI.C.2

Wings Haiku Activity

If you have a good ear for music, you've got a head start at writing haiku.
But even if you're not a music fan, don't worry; it's easy to pick up the rhythm
of this ancient form of Japanese poetry.

Haiku are short poems that don't rhyme, but instead focus on the total number of syllables in each line. Traditional haiku use a total of 17 syllables spread over three lines of text. Most haiku use a formula of 5-7-5: The first and third lines contain 5 syllables and the middle line contains 7. (Some modern haiku use variations on this formula.)

Haiku-Writing Tips

Choose a topic. Nature is the traditional source of inspiration for haiku, but no topics are off limits. What is something that you know or care a lot about? For example, you can write about your pet, your garage band, or your favorite piece of clothing. Get creative!

Consider the message you'd like to deliver. Why write the poem? What's especially interesting about your topic? Try to think of a twist or an unexpected connection for your reader to consider. For instance, you could write about how your basketball team suffered a terrible losing streak of twenty-five games in a row, but then turned things around, made the playoffs, and won the championship.

Follow the formula. Put some words on the page and count the syllables on each line. Change them around until they match the 5-7-5 syllable structure. Reading your words aloud may help you find the right rhythm.

Use a thesaurus. This tool helps you find synonyms (words that have the same definitions as other words) that will allow you to reach your 5-7-5 syllable count. For instance, the word "nice" has one syllable, "friendly" has two syllables, "sociable" has three syllables, and "personable" has four syllables, but all those words can be used interchangeably.

Center it. Once your haiku is complete, center the text on the page (as opposed to aligning it on the left, as you would for an English paper). That's the traditional way of presenting a haiku.

(Shared with permission from Wiener and PowerPoetry.org, 2019)

The term "wings" is used throughout *Enchanted Air,* with varied meanings. Using the Japanese verse form of haiku, teens will write three unrhymed lines of five, seven, and five syllables. A haiku may often feature an image or images, which is meant to depict a moment in time. For this activity, reflect upon one or more of the meanings of "wings" in *Enchanted Air,* using the haiku form.

Curriculum Connections

CCSS.ELA-LITERACY.CCRA.R.2 CCSS.ELA-LITERACY.CCRA.R.4
   CCSS.ELA-LITERACY.CCRA.R.6
CCSS.ELA-LITERACY.CCRA.R.7 CCSS.ELA-LITERACY.CCRA.W.1
   CCSS.ELA-LITERACY.CCRA.W.2
CCSS.ELA-LITERACY.CCRA.W.4 AASL.I.A.2 AASL.I.B.3 AASL.
   II.A.2 AASL.IV.B.4
AASL.V.B.1 AASL.VI.C.2

Jazz Owls: A Novel of the Zoot Suit Riots
by Margarita Engle
Atheneum Books for Young Readers
May 8, 2018
ISBN: 978-1534409439

Grades: 7 and up

Content Tags:
Black, Chinese, Cuban, jazz, Jewish, Latin dancing, Latinx, Mexican, musicians, racism, sailors, swing dancing, USO, war, Zoot Suit Riots

Summary

In Los Angeles in 1942, loose clothes called "zoot suits" were worn to enable movement during swing dances and other Latin dances. During these dancing get-togethers, there were multiple races of people dancing together, which angered some racist sailors, soldiers, and civilians. They responded by rioting and beating the men in zoot suits. The police were no help to the victims—in fact, they blamed and arrested them instead of the perpetrators. "'Isn't this a free country?' one kid asks. 'Can't we wear the kind of clothes that we like?' I find it both newsworthy and sad that he still thinks this is about suits instead of skin."

Jazzed Up Poetry Activity

The Virginia Hamilton Multicultural Literature Conference is held annually at Kent State University in Kent, Ohio. On October 13, 2018, Dr. David Bloome of the Ohio State University was a keynote presenter. Bloome introduced jazz music as a metaphor for reading comprehension. The audience was treated to music samples from Herbie Hancock, Michel Camilo, Mongo Santamaria, and Albert King, and asked to make comparisons among versions of the same song originated by Herbie Hancock in 1962, "Watermelon Man," and covered by the others.

When people listen to jazz, the meaningfulness of their listening is not just in recognizing the musical ideas expressed in the performance, it is in the *total jazz effect:*

- the being there;
- the emotions evoked;
- the distancing and refracting of other worlds in which we live;
- the social relationships we have with others there (in the club dancing, feeling our bodies move together, or at home alone, feeling our bodies move); and
- the way it takes us both into and out of time, and the ways we understand ourselves and others. (Bloome 2018)

Scan these QR codes to listen to the four different jazz versions of "Watermelon Man." Take notes about the various feelings that emerge through the varied interpretations. What is the mood—is it upbeat and happy? Is the rhythm quick or slow? Does it make you want to move? How might you dance to this music? Which instruments do you hear? Which version do you prefer? Then, use your notes to write a free verse poem about "Watermelon Man."

Version 1: Herbie Hancock, via https://www.youtube.com/watch?v=4bjPlBC4h_8 	Version 2: Michel Camilo, via https://www.youtube.com/watch?v=HVhFGumwdBI 
Version 3: Mongo Santamaria, via https://www.youtube.com/watch?v=I43vckpRjMk 	Version 4: Albert King, via https://www.youtube.com/watch?v=6u669AlN5E8 

Curriculum Connections

CCSS.ELA-LITERACY.CCRA.R.7 CCSS.ELA-LITERACY.CCRA.R.9
 CCSS.ELA-LITERACY.CCRA.W.2
CCSS.ELA-LITERACY.CCRA.W.3 CCSS.ELA-LITERACY.
 CCRA.W.4 CCSS.ELA-LITERACY.CCRA.W.8
AASL.I.A.2 AASL.I.C.1 AASL.I. D.3 AASL.II.B.3 AASL.II.D.2 AASL.
 III.C.2 AASL.IV.B.1
AASL.IV.D.2 AASL.V.A.3 AASL.VI.C.2

The Lightning Dreamer: Cuba's Greatest Abolitionist
by Margarita Engle
Harcourt Children's Books
March 31, 2013
ASIN: B00QPH4ZG2

Grades: 7 and up

Content Tags:
abolitionist, arranged marriage, censorship, Cuban, death, equality,
feminism, first love/sex, Latinx, misogyny, performing arts, racism,
rebellion, slavery, violence

Summary

During a time of harsh censorship, daring abolitionists in Cuba were often poets who spoke in metaphors. Gertrudis Gómez de Avellaneda, nicknamed "Tula," was one of these poets. This is her story.

Sonnet Poetry Activity

The Lightning Dreamer takes place during a time when emotions were running high. Poetry was used to express emotion in metaphorical ways. A sonnet can be a perfect style of poetry for expressing strong emotions. There are varied types of sonnets, so for this activity, use the following format. Sonnets are fourteen-line poems with a variable rhyme scheme. There must be three sets of four lines, followed by one set of two lines. The sets of four lines are called quatrains, and the last set of two lines is a couplet. The rhyme scheme is as follows:

First quatrain: ABAB
Second quatrain: CDCD

Third quatrain: EFEF

Couplet: GG

In the style of Cuban abolitionists, be sure to include metaphor in the sonnets.

Curriculum Connections

CCSS.ELA-LITERACY.CCRA.R.2 CCSS.ELA-LITERACY.CCRA.R.4
CCSS.ELA-LITERACY.CCRA.R.6
CCSS.ELA-LITERACY.CCRA.R.7 CCSS.ELA-LITERACY.CCRA.W.1
CCSS.ELA-LITERACY.CCRA.W.2
CCSS.ELA-LITERACY.CCRA.W.4 AASL.I.A.2 AASL.I.B.3 AASL.
II.A.2 AASL.IV.B.4
AASL.V.B.1 AASL.VI.C.2

Soaring Earth by Margarita Engle
Atheneum Books for Young Readers
February 26, 2019
ISBN: 978-1534429536

Grades: 7 and up

Content Tags:
assault, college, coming of age, Cuban American, dating, Latinx, protests, religion, Vietnam War, war

Summary

Soaring Earth picks up at age fourteen, where Margarita Engle's memoir, *Enchanted Air*, left off. In the midst of adolescent struggles and conflict all around her, Margarita finds empowerment via her education, and hope and love in poetry.

Write to Fight Activity

Margarita takes part in protests against the Vietnam War. Although we are not in the Vietnam era, there are other current events that teens may want to protest. One way to protest peacefully is by writing to fight as part of activism. Writing poetry can be a way of using our voices and can provide a sense of empowerment during challenging times. When we write to fight, we are raising our voices against racism, sexism, and xenophobia. Whatever your cause may be: write to fight. Musicians write to fight all the time. Bob Dylan's musical protests became anthems of sorts during the Civil Rights Movement, while modern performers like Kendrick Lamar rap about politics in the hood.

In *Soaring Earth,* Margarita remarks on an interesting derivation in the Spanish language between Mexicans and Cubans. She finds that Mexicans use the term "mira," meaning "look," while Cubanos say "oye," meaning "listen." Both certainly have value individually, but they provide a more dynamic impression when used together. Using both senses of looking and listening in their poems, teens will write a persuasive protest poem about a topic of their choosing. For more resources to accompany this activity, see *Fight the Power: Music as a Social Force,* written by the author of this book for *School Library Journal's Teen Librarian Toolbox,* 2019. It is available at http://www.teenlibrariantoolbox.com/2019/02/fight-the-power-music-as-a-social-force-a-guest-post-by-lisa-krok.

Curriculum Connections

CCSS.ELA-LITERACY.CCRA.R.3 CCSS.ELA-LITERACY.CCRA.R.4 CCSS.ELA-LITERACY.CCRA.R.6
CCSS.ELA-LITERACY.CCRA.R.7 CCSS.ELA-LITERACY.CCRA.W.1 CCSS.ELA-LITERACY.CCRA.W.2
CCSS.ELA-LITERACY.CCRA.W.3 CCSS.ELA-LITERACY.CCRA.W.4 CCSS.ELA-LITERACY.CCRA.W.7
CCSS.ELA-LITERACY.CCRA.W.8 CCSS.ELA-LITERACY.CCRA.W.9 AASL.I.A.2 AASL.I.B.3
AASL.I.D.1 AASL.I.D.3 AASL.II.B.2 AASL.II.C.2 AASL.III.C.2 AASL.III.D.2 AASL.IV.D.2
AASL.V.A.2 AASL.V.B.1 AASL.V.C.1 AASL.VI.C.2

With a Star in My Hand: Ruben Dario, Poetry Hero
by Margarita Engle
Atheneum Books for Young Readers
February 18, 2020
ISBN: 978-1534424937

Grades: 7 and up

Content Tags:
adoption, alcoholism, courage, death, family dynamics, family secrets, hope, Indigenous, Latinx, library, natural disasters, Nicaraguan, poverty

Summary

After a farmer finds him abandoned as a small boy in a cow pasture, Ruben is adopted by his great-uncle and his wife. He does not know what happened to his Mama. Self-taught to read at three years old, Ruben learns to trade rhymes for treats, and he reads to improve his rhymes. As he experiences falling in love, heartbreak, family secrets, natural disasters, smallpox, poverty, drinking, and travel, poetry is always where he finds hope, the star in his hand.

Redondilla Poetry Activity

One type of poetry that Ruben wrote was redondilla. This is a Spanish verse form in which each stanza consists of four lines, each with eight syllables, and a rhyme scheme.

A

B

B

A

This means that the first and last lines will rhyme, and the second and third lines will rhyme. For even more of a challenge, try an octavilla, which is a poem of eight lines consisting of two redondillas, which share rhymes. Think you are all that, as Ruben does? Try writing a decima. There are various versions, and this one is popular in Puerto Rico. It is a 10-liner with 8 syllables per line, in the following rhyme pattern:

A

B

B

A

A

C

C

D

D

C

Still going strong? The last challenge is a seguidilla. This is a Spanish form of verse that has seven lines of counted syllables in the sequence 7, 5, 7, 5, 5, 7, 5.

The rhymes occur at the second and fourth, and the fifth and seventh lines. This pattern would be:

X

A

X

A

B

X

B

If you made it this far, congratulations! You might just be a poetry hero like Ruben Dario.

Curriculum Connections

CCSS.ELA-LITERACY.CCRA.R.2 CCSS.ELA-LITERACY.CCRA.R.4
    CCSS.ELA-LITERACY.CCRA.R.6
CCSS.ELA-LITERACY.CCRA.R.7 CCSS.ELA-LITERACY.CCRA.W.1
    CCSS.ELA-LITERACY.CCRA.W.2
CCSS.ELA-LITERACY.CCRA.W.4 4 AASL.I.A.2 AASL.I.B.3 AASL.
    II.A.2 AASL.IV.B.4
AASL.V.B.1 AASL.VI.C.2

The Good Braider by Terry Farish
Skyscape
May 1, 2012
ISBN: 978-0761462675

Grades: 9 and up

Content Tags:
braiding, Christian, coming of age, cultural traditions, death, grief, Muslim, physical abuse, refugees, sexual assault/abuse, Sudan, torn between cultures/places, tradition, war

Summary

Viola flees war-torn Sudan with some of her family members and settles in Portland, Maine. As she acclimates to an American way of life, such as wearing a shorter skirt or dating a boy, she feels in conflict with her very traditional mother. While Viola straddles a life built on two cultures, she learns ways to braid together the strands of her old life with those of her new one.

Braided Poems Activity

Because braiding is a tradition in Viola's life, try to write braided poems! Here is a format that author Cynthia Harrison (2012) uses as a guide:

Thread 1

1. Ground the poem in a common experience that you know enough about that you can dig into it.
2. List everyday activities, and then break those down into smaller bits.

Here's an example from my list: Cleaning: silver polishing, cat box, closet. I ended up with seven common experiences and had three or four specific kinds of general activity. Lots to choose from.

Thread 2

3. This part is about emotional relationship issues, yours or some-one else's or imagined, The emotion can be joyous or devastating, an argument, a moment of peace, a death, a birth. Things that can be the emotional tie to the concrete activity in the first thread.
4. Brainstorm a list of names that have emotional connections for you, with some comments after a few of them.
5. Choose grounded common experience and person with emo-tional resonance. Write lines expressing both these things, not necessarily in a linear narrative form.

Curriculum Connections

CCSS.ELA-LITERACY.CCRA.R.2 CCSS.ELA-LITERACY.CCRA.R.4
   CCSS.ELA-LITERACY.CCRA.R.5
CCSS.ELA-LITERACY.CCRA.R.6 CCSS.ELA-LITERACY.CCRA.R.7
   CCSS.ELA-LITERACY.CCRA.W.2
CCSS.ELA-LITERACY.CCRA.W.3 CCSS.ELA-LITERACY.
   CCRA.W.4 AASL.I.A.2 AASL.I.B.3
AASL.III.C.2 AASL.IV.B.4 AASL.IV.D.2 AASL.VI. C.2

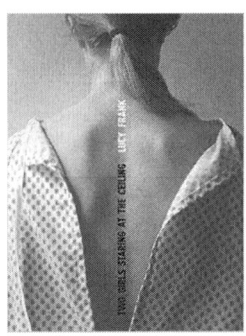

Two Girls Staring at the Ceiling **by Lucy Frank**
Schwartz & Wade
August 5, 2014
ISBN: 978-0307979742

Grades 7 and up

Content Tags:
autoimmune, Crohn's disease, hospitals, IBD, teen pregnancy/teen mothers

Summary

Two girls share a hospital room and an illness, in very opposite ways. Where one is quiet, the other is loud. Where one is polite, the other is rude. One screams in pain, while the other silently tolerates it. As their friendship slowly grows, the curtain separating their hospital beds opens, but is one is getting better while the other declines?

Exquisite Corpse Poetry Activity

The unique thing about this book is the format of the line running down the middle of the page, which is a metaphor for the curtain between the girls in their hospital room. This has a similar feel to a parlor game created in the 1920s during the Parisian Surrealist Movement. Exquisite corpse poetry actually has nothing at all to do with corpses, but the name is certainly intriguing to teens! Players would create lines of poetry randomly by passing their papers around the group. Oddly, one of the lines created back then was: "The exquisite corpse will drink the young wine," which is how the game got its name!

Exquisite corpse is a collaborative poetry game played by several people, each of whom writes a word on a sheet of paper, folds the paper to conceal it, and passes it on to the next player for his or her contribution. It is a good idea to have participants agree on a sentence structure before beginning. An example might be *adjective, noun, verb, adjective, noun*. Small adjustments like verb tenses and articles can be configured after the poem has been written by the group.

Another option instead of each poet writing just a single word is to show a photo or painting, choose from a list of simple topics, or play music for inspiration. Teens write a line of poetry based upon given criteria, such as number of syllables, word count, or structure. They should fold the paper over so the next poet cannot see it, and then pass it on. Keep passing until everyone has had a chance to contribute at least one time (more for smaller groups).

Afterward, open them up and read the poems that were created. There are unlimited ways to play this game over and over by altering the criteria, switching groups, or other modifications. Exquisite corpse is a fun way to collaborate with other poets. The only real hard-and-fast rule is that each poet cannot see what the others have written. This can produce a surprising, hilarious, and sometimes completely absurd poem (Poets.org 2004).

Curriculum Connections

CCSS.ELA-LITERACY.CCRA.R.3 CCSS.ELA-LITERACY.CCRA.R.5
    CCSS.ELA-LITERACY.CCRA.R.6
CCSS.ELA-LITERACY.CCRA.R.7 CCSS.ELA-LITERACY.CCRA.W.3
    CCSS.ELA-LITERACY.CCRA.W.4
AASL.I.A.2 AASL.I.B.3 AASL.I.C.1 AASL.C.4 AASL.II.C.2 AASL.
    III.A.2 AASL.III.D.1
AASL.IV.B.2 AASL.IV.B.4 AASL.V. C.3 AASL.VI.C.2

Resources for Crohn's Disease and IBD

Crohn's and Colitis Foundation
https://www.crohnscolitisfoundation.org/what-is-crohns-disease

AGA (American Gastroenterological Association)
https://www.gastro.org/practice-guidance/gi-patient-center/topic/inflammatory
    -bowel-disease-ibd

Between the Lines by Nikki Grimes
Nancy Paulsen Books
February 13, 2018
ISBN: 978-0399246883

Grades: 7 and up

Content Tags:
alcoholism, Black, Chinese, drugs, foster care, immigrants, journalism, open mic, outcast, poverty, Puerto Rican, self-esteem, slam poetry, teachers, Vietnamese, writing

Summary

This companion novel in verse to Grimes's *Bronx Masquerade* shows how poetry can connect us with not only others, but also ourselves. The story is told in a hybrid of prose and verse, as Darrian and his classmates bond over their poetry as they get to know each other by the shared experiences of their struggles and differences, which emerge through their writing.

6 TIPS FOR USING MULTIMEDIA TO ENHANCE YOUR POEMS

We all know that writing poetry is an amazing, creative way to express ourselves, but have you ever thought about what you can do with your poems after you have written them? There is so much technology that surrounds us every day, so why not put it to use? Combining our poems with different forms of multimedia is a fun way to take our poetry to the next level.

Video: Try using your phone, computer, or camera to record a video of yourself reading one of your poems. This way, people can actually hear you speak your own words, and the emotions of the poem will come across much stronger than if people were to simply read your poem themselves.

Slam: You might have been part of an online poetry slam, but have you ever been to one in person? Well, why not plan your own? Decide on an issue that is important to you, invite a bunch of your friends to read poetry they have written about that issue, and record a video of yourselves doing so. You will have created your own live poetry slam, and once the video is ready, you can edit it and add components like background music.

Voice: Nervous about being seen on camera but still want people to hear you read your own poetry? No problem! You can use a microphone connected to your computer, or even your cell phone, to record yourself reading your poems. Using your own voice will definitely add a new dimension to your poem! Check out how these poets use their voices to contribute an extra layer to their work.

Microsoft PowerPoint: You may have used the PowerPoint program to make presentations for school, but have you ever thought about combining it with your poetry? You can put the text of one of your poems on different slides and add pictures that match the words. These pictures can be ones you find online or that you take yourself.

Song: Turn your poem into a song, or to take that one step further—a music video. You can take a video of yourself singing your poem to music you have recorded, or you can even get up and dance!

(Shared with permission from Wiener and PowerPoetry.org, 2019)

Curriculum Connections

> CCSS.ELA-LITERACY.CCRA.R.2 CCSS.ELA-LITERACY.CCRA.R.4
>   CCSS.ELA-LITERACY.CCRA.R.7
> CCSS.ELA-LITERACY.CCRA.W.3 CCSS.ELA-LITERACY.
>   CCRA.W.4 CCSS.ELA-LITERACY.CCRA.W.6
> CCSS.ELA-LITERACY.CCRA.W.8 AASL.I.B.3 AASL I.C.4 AASL.
>   II.B.1 AASL II.C.2 AASL. II.D.2
> AASL.III.D.1. AASL.IV.D.2 AASL.V.B.1 AASL.VI.C.2

Grimes adds an author's note at the end of the book about the character Jenesis Whyte, who was in foster care and in danger as she was aging out of the system. A former foster child herself, Grimes describes disheartening statistics: 50 percent to 70 percent of those aging out are homeless, 25 percent of these young men are incarcerated, and a rate of pregnancy in these young women is six times the rate of women under twenty-one who had not aged out of foster care.

Grimes lists some resources for newly aged-out former foster kids to help get them on their feet. For instance, Inspire Life Skills Training, Inc. offers critical assistance to former foster kids in need. Services that they provide include affordable housing, education/job training, life skills training, part-time employment, mentoring, and access to professional counseling and medical care.

The following organizations can provide a hand-up for help:

www.inspirelifeskills.org

www.coventanthouse.org

www.theteenproject.com

www.alternativesforgirls.org

www.agingoutinstititute.org

www.childrenscabinet.org

www.beconinterfaith.org

www.communityyouthservices.org

www.y2yharvardsquare.org

www.fosterclub.com

These links and others are also accessible on Grimes's website, www.nikkigrimes.com.

Bronx Masquerade by Nikki Grimes
Dial Books
December 31, 2002
ISBN: 978-0803725690

Grades: 7 and up

Content Tags:
atheists, Black, body image, cancer, death, design, domestic violence, drawing, dyslexia, friendships, Harlem Renaissance, Italian, Jewish, music, open mic, outcast, overdose, painting, poverty, Puerto Rican, racism, slam poetry, teachers, teen pregnancy/teen mothers, theater

Summary

After Wesley Boone's English class reads poetry from the Harlem Renaissance, it sparks an interest in writing poetry among the students. Wesley is the first to read his aloud, and then others in the class begin volunteering. The weekly poetry sessions soon evolve as an outlet of sorts for the group, as they reveal their inner thoughts about each other and themselves. In doing so, they uncover what lives behind the eyes, beneath the skin, and beyond the masquerade.

Cypher Poetry Activity

Mr. Ward's school assignment evolves into poetry via open mic, and Wesley's classmates bring their own topics and concerns to the mic. The emotions presented in open mic poetry sometimes progress into poetry slams.

Scan this QR code for a brief video of a cypher circle of poets (Young Audience Arts for Learning NJ & Eastern PA 2017). https://www.youtube.com/watch?v=hFyBURoUSE4.

A *cypher* is a group of poets who take turns picking up and adding on to the poetry from the person before them; or, in a poetry slam, a circle of poets who take turns reciting poems, which can expand into a hip-hop freestyle battle.

Cypher poetry is very open ended and can be written or spoken. The key is to keep going and not break the circle. Pass the paper or pass the mic. Try it on paper first to become comfortable and create a rhythm of sorts, then advance into an open mic version. For more on slam poetry, see Elizabeth Acevedo in the Author/Title Index.

Curriculum Connections

CCSS.ELA-LITERACY.CCRA.R.3 CCSS.ELA-LITERACY.CCRA.R.4
CCSS.ELA-LITERACY.CCRA.R.5
CCSS.ELA-LITERACY.CCRA.R.6 CCSS.ELA-LITERACY.CCRA.R.7
CCSS.ELA-LITERACY.CCRA.W.3
CCSS.ELA-LITERACY.CCRA.W.4 CCSS.ELA-LITERACY.
CCRA.W.8 AASL.I.B.3 AASL I.C.4
AASL.II.B.1 AASL II.C.2 AASL. II.D.2 AASL.III.D.1. AASL.IV.D.2
AASL.V.B.1 AASL.VI.C.2

Garvey's Choice by Nikki Grimes
Wordsong
October 4, 2016
ISBN: 978-1629797403

Grades: 4–8

Content Tags:
Black, body image, bookworm, choir, music, parental expectations, sports

Summary

Garvey's dad wants him to be athletic like his sister and into sports, but Garvey prefers *Star Trek,* books, music, and math. He feels like a big disappointment to his father until they uncover their common love of music and singing. Then they are able to make a connection.

Tanka Poetry Activity

The ancient Japanese poetry form known as *tanka* is a poem written in thirty-one syllables, traditionally in a single, unbroken line. A form of waka, Japanese song or verse, *tanka* translates as "short song," and is better known in its five-line, 5/7/5/7/7 syllable count form. Grimes uses the ancient Japanese poetry form, tanka, in this book. The word *tanka* also translates as "short poem" in Japanese. A line-by-line syllable count can vary in modern English versions, but the number of lines in a basic tanka remains the same, at five lines long. Not every poet follows a syllable count, but Grimes approaches the syllable count like a puzzle, where she tries to find the piece that fits best. Tanka poems can often focus on mood and also may include telling a story, as in *Garvey's Choice*. Try this modern form of tanka used in this book:

Line 1: 5 syllables

Line 2: 7 syllables

Line 3: 5 syllables

Line 4: 7 syllables

Line 5: 7 syllables

Curriculum Connections

CCSS.ELA-LITERACY.CCRA.R.2 CCSS.ELA-LITERACY.CCRA.R.4
CCSS.ELA-LITERACY.CCRA.R.6
CCSS.ELA-LITERACY.CCRA.R.7 CCSS.ELA-LITERACY.CCRA.W.1
CCSS.ELA-LITERACY.CCRA.W.2
CCSS.ELA-LITERACY.CCRA.W.4 AASL.I.A.2 AASL.I.B.3 AASL.
II.A.2 AASL.IV.B.4
AASL.V.B.1 AASL.VI.C.2

***Ordinary Hazards: A Memoir* by Nikki Grimes**
Wordsong
October 8, 2019
ISBN: 978-1629798813

Grades: 7 and up

Content Tags:
alcoholism, assault, asthma, Black, books, death, encouragement, family dynamics, foster care, grief, Harlem, library, mental illness, molestation, performing arts, prayers/faith, puberty, racism, sexual assault/abuse, teachers, writing

Summary

Nikki and her sister, Carol, live with their mentally ill mother after their father leaves. When alcoholism and schizophrenia combine to make their mother unfit, Nikki and Carol are placed in foster care and eventually separated. Three years later, Mom remarries and Nikki returns to her care, which includes a new, nefarious stepfather. Throughout the trials of an unstable home life, Nikki makes the library her new best friend, and she finds encouragement from her teacher and her inconsistent father, who has come back into her life. The epilogue at the end tells of one of Nikki's inspirations, James Baldwin, and how she connected with him to read her poetry.

Diamante Poetry Activity

Nikki loved the library growing up. It was a safe space for her during times when stability at home was questionable. She found that books, words, writing, and poetry helped her make sense of life. The library is many things to many people.

A diamante is a poem of seven lines that does not rhyme. The first and last lines are the shortest, while the lines in the middle are longer, and the lines are centered, which

Scan this QR code for a brief video from the Brooklyn Public Library (BPLvideos 2011), highlighting the varied things patrons love: https://www .youtube.com/watch?v=SCagg1FRU68.

gives diamante poems a diamond shape. Because *diamante* is the Italian word for *diamond*, these poems are named for their rhombus shape. Libraries were a shining diamond in young Nikki's life, so this form seems fitting to accompany *Ordinary Hazards*.

Kenn Nesbitt (2011) advises the following rules for diamantes:

Diamantes are seven lines long.

The first and last lines have just one word.

The second and sixth lines have two words.

The third and fifth lines have three words.

And the fourth line has four words.

Lines 1, 4, and 7 have nouns.

Lines 2 and 6 have adjectives.

Lines 3 and 5 have verbs.

Here's an easy way to visualize all three rules:

Noun
Adj., Adj.
Verb, Verb, Verb
Noun, Noun, Noun, Noun

Verb, Verb, Verb

Adj., Adj.

Noun

There are two types of these poems: synonym diamantes and antonym diamantes. In a synonym diamante, the nouns in the first and last lines mean
basically the same thing. In an antonym diamante, the nouns in the first and
last lines are opposites. Before getting started writing a diamante, the poet
needs to decide the topic they are writing about and if they are creating synonym or antonym diamantes. Once that is determined, simply make a list of
words that are related, including nouns, adjectives, and verbs. Remember that
the thesaurus is your friend to help find alternative words as synonyms and
antonyms. Also, centering your poem in the middle of the page helps make
the diamond shape more apparent. The first time students try the diamante
format, assign the topic of "Libraries." After they practice with this one, future
diamantes can be a topic of each person's choice.

Curriculum Connections

CCSS.ELA-LITERACY.CCRA.R.2 CCSS.ELA-LITERACY.CCRA.R.4
    CCSS.ELA-LITERACY.CCRA.R.6
CCSS.ELA-LITERACY.CCRA.R.7 CCSS.ELA-LITERACY.CCRA.W.1
    CCSS.ELA-LITERACY.CCRA.W.2
CCSS.ELA-LITERACY.CCRA.W.4 AASL.I.A.2 AASL.I.B.3 AASL.
    II.A.2 AASL.IV.B.4 AASL.V.B.1
AASL.VI.C.2

House Arrest by K. A. Holt
Chronicle Books
October 6, 2015
ISBN: 978-1452134772

Grades: 6 and up

Content Tags:
family dynamics, hospitals, house arrest, journaling,
probation, serious illness

Summary

Tim never thought he would be on house arrest for the next year. He thought
probation was something that happened to other kids, not to him. As he
checks in weekly with both a therapist and a probation officer, he keeps a

journal. After his father leaves, Tim takes it upon himself to assist his mom financially and help with his sickly baby brother Levi, all while chronicling his thoughts in his journal.

Poetry Journal Activity

Writing in a journal can be a way of releasing stress on the page. Tim attends therapy as part of his probation, and he keeps track of his feelings in a journal. "A journal is a place to express yourself, to record your thoughts, feelings and observations, and to cultivate your poetic style. The cool thing about your journal is that it's yours. You can keep it secret or share it with your friends and family. You might even read some of your poetry out loud at a talent show or poetry jam. Whatever you decide to do with it, a daily poetry journal will keep you writing. And the more you write, the better writer you become!" (Nesbitt 2016).

Nesbitt has these suggestions for having kids write poetry in journals:

*   Choose a journal that fits your style.

    To keep words neat and in order, a spiral or other lined notebook is suggested. For those who like to draw or doodle around their poems, blank pages are recommended. Writing on the go when you feel inspired can be achieved by using a smaller book that you can fit into a pocket or purse.

*   Organize your journal.

    One way to set up your journal is by topic. You can use sticky notes or other page tabs to find locations easily. Some prefer to keep everything chronological, simply dating the top of each page. Others may organize by type of poetic form, such as clerihew, haiku, concrete, free verse, cinquain, tanka, acrostic, and others. However you choose to arrange your journal, it needs to work for you.

*   Write—and keep writing.

    Keep a routine for writing a bit each day. It might be on a bus ride home, before bed, while listening to music, or any time that works for you. Find your writing time and make it your own oasis.

Curriculum Connections

CCSS.ELA-LITERACY.CCRA.R.3 CCSS.ELA-LITERACY.CCRA.W.2
CCSS.ELA-LITERACY.CCRA.W.3
CCSS.ELA-LITERACY.CCRA.W.4 CCSS.ELA-LITERACY.
CCRA.W.10 AASL.I.B.3 AASL.I.D.3
AASL.II.D.3 AASL.III.C.2 AASL.V.A.2 AASL.V.C.1 AASL.VI.

Knock Out by **K. A. Holt**
Chronicle Books
March 6, 2018
ISBN: 978-1452163581

Grades: 5–8

Content Tags:
boxing, divorce, family dynamics, health issues, journaling

Summary

Knock Out picks up as a companion book to *House Arrest*, this time from Levi's point of view. Because he had been a very sickly baby with serious respiratory issues, his mom and brother are overprotective and consider him damaged. When the father who abandoned him years ago comes back into the picture, Levi grabs the chance to try boxing and reinvent himself in the eyes of his family.

Releasing Anger and Stress Poetry Activity

Anger and stress can be released physically, such as through boxing, or emotionally, via writing, talking, and other communicative activities. Levi's older brother, Tim, began writing in a journal when he was on house arrest, so Levi decides to try that as a way of putting all his anger into the notebook instead of keeping it in his head.

Start by making a list of emotions that you connect with. They might be things that you have experienced firsthand, or injustices to someone else that you have heard about. Let your thoughts flow for a few minutes and write down as many emotions as you can. You may find that your list includes a wide range of emotions. That is just fine—this is your own personal experience.

Next, choose the one that speaks most to you and highlight or circle it. Using that word as a springboard, take some time to write in free verse about whatever comes to mind. You could also write about a personal experience when you felt that emotion. Poetry is personal, and it is okay to keep your poem private if you prefer not to share. Remember that the arrangement, font, size, color, bold, italics, and capitalization of your words also can also help convey meaning. For example, if I have a migraine, I wouldn't write about having an ordinary "headache." I would write I have a "**HEAD. ACHE**." When you are finished writing, read your poem to yourself or share it aloud. Remember to accentuate any words with specialized font as described previously.

Curriculum Connections

CCSS.ELA-LITERACY.CCRA.R.3 CCSS.ELA-LITERACY.CCRA.W.2
   CCSS.ELA-LITERACY.CCRA.W.3
CCSS.ELA-LITERACY.CCRA.W.4 CCSS.ELA-LITERACY.
   CCRA.W.10 AASL.I.B.3 AASL.I.D.3
AASL.II.D.3 AASL.III.C.2 AASL.V.A.2 AASL.V.C.1 AASL.VI.

Redwood and Ponytail by K. A. Holt
Chronicle Books
October 1, 2019
ISBN: 978-1452172880

Grades: 5 and up

Content Tags:
cheerleading, coming out, LGBTQ+, mascot,
parental expectations, school election, self-
acceptance, sports, volleyball

Summary

Kate's mom is pushing for her to be captain of the cheerleading squad, but Kate prefers being the mascot. When she befriends Tam, she begins questioning her sexuality. When Kate's mom shuts down her revelation, she seeks validation from her sister, who happens to be estranged from her mother.

Sorry, Not Sorry Poem Activity

Kate prefers being the team mascot to the cheerleader her mom wants her to be. She is attracted to girls, not boys—and she is not sorry about it.

Sorry, Not Sorry poetry stemmed from the poem "This Is Just to Say" by William Carlos Williams. When reading the first part of the poem, we see him appearing to apologize for eating someone else's plums. As we continue to the end of the poem, though, the reader realizes he is in fact not sorry.

Encourage students to think of something in the past they apologized for but were not sincere about it. Following the format of the Williams poem, have students write their own versions of Sorry, Not Sorry poetry. Choose volunteers to share aloud, which often results in a lot of laughs.

Williams's original poem can be found at https://poets.org/poem/just -say.

Curriculum Connections

CCSS.ELA-LITERACY.CCRA.R.1 CCSS.ELA-LITERACY.CCRA.R.2
  CCSS.ELA-LITERACY.CCRA.R.3
CCSS.ELA-LITERACY.CCRA.R.4 CCSS.ELA-LITERACY.CCRA.R.5
  CCSS.ELA-LITERACY.CCRA.R.6
CCSS.ELA-LITERACY.CCRA.R.7 CCSS.ELA-LITERACY.CCRA.W.3
  CCSS.ELA-LITERACY.CCRA.W.4
AASL.I.A.2 AASL.I.B.3 AASL.I.D.3 AASL.II.B.3 AASL.III.C.2 AASL.
  IV.B.2 AASL.IV.B.4
AASL.IV.D.2 AASL.V.B.1 AASL.B.C.2

Crank by Ellen Hopkins
Margaret K. McElderry Books
June 15, 2010
ISBN: 978-1416995135

Grades: 9 and up

Content Tags:
addiction, divorce, drugs, first love/sex, self-harm,
sexual assault/abuse, teen pregnancy/teen
mothers

Summary

Although this book is not about a beast or a dragon, it involves a monster.
The destructive, life changing monster that is crystal meth snatches Kristina,
and she transforms into her brash alter-ego, Bree. Based upon the author's own
daughter and her addiction to crystal meth, this realistically portrays the hold
that meth has on an addict.

Addiction Recovery Poetry Journal Activity

Benefits of Writing in Addiction Recovery—Most people have no problem accepting the claim that talking about problems can be a great help.
This is reflected in the much loved quote, a problem shared is a problem
halved. What is less widely appreciated is the idea that writing about things
can also be highly therapeutic . . . trauma and mental health issues can ren-
der a person voiceless, literally and figuratively. Addicts sometimes abuse
chemical substances in order to find a voice even if it is not their own . . .
Writing can assist you in finding your own voice and be very edifying. You
do not have to share your work in order to begin appreciating your unique

view on life. Writing poetry will help you to build strength and confidence in your natural sober self. (Bridges, 2014)

Poetry journals seem like the best option for this sort of journey, to evolve and track progress. Kenn Nesbitt (2016) has these suggestions for writing poetry in journals:

- Choose a journal that fits your style.

  To keep words neat and in order, a spiral or other lined notebook is suggested. For those who like to draw or doodle around their poems, blank pages are recommended. Writing on the go when you feel inspired can be achieved using a smaller book that you can fit into a pocket or purse.

- Organize your journal.

  One way to set up your journal is by topics. You can use sticky notes or other page tabs to find locations easily. Some prefer to keep everything chronological, simply dating the top of each page. Others may organize by type of poetic form, such as clerihew, haiku, concrete, free verse, cinquain, tanka, acrostic, and others. However you choose to arrange your journal, it needs to work for you.

- Write—and keep writing.

  Keep a routine for writing a bit each day. It might be on a bus ride home, before bed, while listening to music, or any time that works for you. Find your writing time and make it your own oasis.

Curriculum Connections

CCSS.ELA-LITERACY.CCRA.R.3 CCSS.ELA-LITERACY.CCRA.W.2
  CCSS.ELA-LITERACY.CCRA.W.3
CCSS.ELA-LITERACY.CCRA.W.4 CCSS.ELA-LITERACY.
  CCRA.W.10 AASL.I.B.3 AASL.I.D.3
AASL.II.D.3 AASL.III.C.2 AASL.V.A.2 AASL.V.C.1 AASL.VI.

Resources for Addiction

SAMHSA (Substance Abuse and Mental Health Services Administration)
Visit www.samhsa.gov/find-help/national-helpline or call SAMHSA's National Helpline at 800-662-HELP (4357)

National Drug Helpline (844-289-0879)
http://drughelpline.org/meth-hotline

Glass (Crank #2) by Ellen Hopkins
Margaret K. McElderry Books
August 21, 2007
ISBN: 978-1416940906

Grades: 9 and up

Content Tags:
addiction, custody, drugs, family dynamics, jail, sex, teen pregnancy/teen mothers

Summary

Now that Kristina has a baby to take care of, she is determined to call the shots. However, the monster—crystal, crank, glass, whatever you call it—will not let go and once again has seized Kristina in its tortured grasp. Even her baby is not enough to make her stop, in this haunting and disturbing view into addiction and the effects that it has on a family.

Cinquain Poetry Activity

Crystal meth is known by many names throughout this series. *Crank, glass, monster, crystal*—whatever you call it, it ruins lives. Cinquain poems are similar to other Japanese poetic forms like haiku and tanka. They are five lines long, with a syllable pattern of 2, 4, 6, 8, 2. They sometimes rhyme, but usually they do not.

A didactic cinquain is a specific kind of cinquain, which follows the pattern given here:

> Line 1: One word, usually a noun, which also serves as the title of the poem
>
> Line 2: Two adjectives describing the title
>
> Line 3: Three verbs that show action
>
> Line 4: A short sentence that show emotions about the poem's subject
>
> Line 5: A one-word synonym of the title

Try writing cinquains with the standard 2, 4, 5, 8, 2 syllable pattern; and when you are ready for a challenge, add in the didactic cinquain criteria. You can write your poem about crystal meth, heroin, or any other substance that brings to mind strong feelings.

Curriculum Connections

CCSS.ELA-LITERACY.CCRA.R.2 CCSS.ELA-LITERACY.CCRA.R.4
CCSS.ELA-LITERACY.CCRA.R.6

CCSS.ELA-LITERACY.CCRA.R.7 CCSS.ELA-LITERACY.CCRA.W.1
 CCSS.ELA-LITERACY.CCRA.W.2
CCSS.ELA-LITERACY.CCRA.W.4 AASL.I.A.2 AASL.I.B.3 AASL.
 II.A.2 AASL.IV.B.4 AASL.V.B.1
AASL.VI.C.2

Resources for Addiction

SAMHSA (Substance Abuse and Mental Health Services Administration)
Visit www.samhsa.gov/find-help/national-helpline or call SAMHSA's National
 Helpline at 800-662-HELP (4357)

National Drug Helpline (844-289-0879)
http://drughelpline.org/meth-hotline

Fallout (Crank #3) by Ellen Hopkins
Margaret K. McElderry Books
September 14, 2010
ISBN: 978-1416950097

Grades: 9 and up

Content Tags:
addiction, alcoholism, college, drugs, family
dynamics, foster care, homelessness, hope, OCD,
teen pregnancy/teen mothers

Summary

Book three of the *Crank* series picks up with Kristina's oldest son, Hunter, at age nineteen. Three of Kristina's five children are living with different guardians in different homes with different last names. With disgruntled feelings toward the mother who barely even knows them, the children have been born with a predisposition for addiction after Kristina's twenty-year high. The three viewpoints of Kristina's children spell out the fact that addiction is never just one person's problem.

Viewpoints Poetry Activity

Choose the viewpoint of one of Kristina's three children and write a poem in the style of that person to Kristina about how her actions have affected your life.

Curriculum Connections

CCSS.ELA-LITERACY.CCRA.R.3 CCSS.ELA-LITERACY.CCRA.R.6
    CCSS.ELA-LITERACY.CCRA.R.8
CCSS.ELA-LITERACY.CCRA.W.3 CCSS.ELA-LITERACY.
    CCRA.W.4 AASL.I.A.2 AASL.I.B.3
AASL.I.D.3 AASL.II.B.3 AASL.III.C.2 AASL.IV.B.2 AASL.IV.B.4
    AASL.IV.D.2
AASL.V.B.1 AASL.B.C.2

Resources for Families and Friends of Alcoholics and Addicts

Al-Anon Family Groups—Offering hope and help for families and friends of
    alcoholics
https://al-anon.org

Nar-Anon Family Groups—Designed to help families and friends of addicts
https://www.nar-anon.org

Some Girls Bind by **Rory James**
Enslow Publishers
February 1, 2019
ISBN: 978-1538382530

Grades: 7 and up *[can be used as high interest–low-level (hi-lo) for older teens]*

Content Tags:
alcoholism, binding, coming out, family dynamics,
LGBTQ+

Summary

Jamie has been keeping a secret . . . she binds her chest each day to feel more like herself. She is questioning why she does this, and she feels she isn't like other girls. She is afraid to tell her friends that she is genderqueer, but she finds some solace in her brother's support.

LGBTQ+ Advocacy Poetry Activity

Jamie kept her secret for a long time because she was afraid of what the reaction would be from her friends and family. Everyone deserves to become their most honest and authentic self. Gender roles often put people in boxes that don't conform to their true identities. Understanding that gender is a social structure that operates on a spectrum is the first step in challenging gender expectations. Understanding that people are free to identify themselves however they choose would follow soon after. The next step, of course, is picking up a pen and creating some change.

Become an Ally. Being an ally means you are the support for a group you may not identify with directly. An ally's job is to create the space for the marginalized body to talk and express themselves. They offer assistance and make sure that they listen to the needs of those who are facing injustices. Think of it like this: the ally helps set the stage so that those who've felt marginalized can take the microphone and speak their truth.

Write from Understanding. Even if someone's experience is different from your own, you can still gather an understanding of the trials they face. There are great organizations—like GLAAD and Trans Youth Equality—where you can educate yourself on the different work being done to ensure the safety and rights of trans citizens.

Advocacy Is Activism. Your poetry speaks volumes! By writing for the marginalized, you're revealing their narrative to a broader community of people. Most people don't identify with something unless it has influence on their own experience. Using your poetry, you can introduce these people to injustices that they have never been aware of. Open mics are hives of diversity where several different narratives are shared. In this way, poetry can start conversations that live off of the stage.

Imagining a Better World. Through our literary imagination, we can create a world better than the one we live in: one where people are treated the same regardless of their sexual orientation or gender preference. Challenge yourself to write poems where the gender of the speaker is never clear. Disassociate the genders from the actions in order to prove that men and women can do many of the same things—or that you don't have to identify as a man or woman at all. Write an ode to your transgendered peers who are brave enough to be themselves, or write a love story where neither of the characters adhere to gender norms. One of the most effective ways to advocate for others is to draw normative, positive attention simply by including a new perspective in your writing.

(Shared with permission from Wiener and PowerPoetry.org)

Scan this QR code for a video of spoken word poetry for trans rights (Yale's Voke Spoken Word Group 2017). https://www.youtube.com /watch?v=1bcgXyc5nm8.

Using the "I pledge allegiance" prompt performed in the video, students will write free verse advocacy poetry (for trans rights or any other topic they feel passionate about). If they wish to perform it as spoken word poetry as was done in the video, they can collaborate in groups of two or three.

Curriculum Connections

CCSS.ELA-LITERACY.CCRA.R.3 CCSS.ELA-LITERACY.CCRA.R.4
 CCSS.ELA-LITERACY.CCRA.R.6
CCSS.ELA-LITERACY.CCRA.R.7 CCSS.ELA-LITERACY.CCRA.W.1
 CCSS.ELA-LITERACY.CCRA.W.2
CCSS.ELA-LITERACY.CCRA.W.3 CCSS.ELA-LITERACY.
 CCRA.W.4 CCSS.ELA-LITERACY.CCRA.W.7
CCSS.ELA-LITERACY.CCRA.W.8 CCSS.ELA-LITERACY.
 CCRA.W.9 AASL.I.A.2 AASL.I.B.3
AASL.I.D.1 AASL.I.D.3 AASL.II.B.2 AASL.II.C.2 AASL.III.C.2
 AASL.III.D.2 AASL.IV.D.2
AASL.V.A.2 AASL.V.B.1 AASL.V.C.1 AASL.VI.C.2

A FEW IMPORTANT TIPS FOR ENGAGING WITH TRANSGENDER TEENS

Respect the names and pronouns transgender youth have chosen for themselves. If you don't know—ask. Model that respect in front of all students and colleagues.

The experiences of LGBT youth vary greatly. Lumping LGBT experiences together is a mistake. For example, transgender and gender-nonconforming youth often face more hostility and bullying at school than their lesbian, gay and bisexual peers.

Supportive school staff can make all the difference. One educator can make a difference—but the goal is building an inclusive and welcoming school.

All students have the right to use the bathroom that corresponds to their gender identity. A transgender student should never be forced to use alternative facilities to make other students comfortable.

Mentorship is instrumental for trans students' success. When possible, seek out or establish a trans-to-trans mentorship program for students. Adult mentors can serve as a crucial support system for trans students and provide models for what it looks like to live life as a transgender person.

Curriculum and instruction play a big part in supporting trans youth. Including transgender figures and narratives in the curriculum helps ensure that trans students do not feel alone. Paying attention to and affirming non-gender-binary identities in student work is also very important.

Always trust and defer to transgender youth. If you are a non-trans-identified adult, don't question what your trans student is going through. Follow their lead and provide your continued support along the way.

Be aware of bias—your own and others'. Uncover any transphobia and personal bias you may hold. Learn to recognize and interrupt gender-identity-based bullying and harassment.

(Reprinted with permission of Teaching Tolerance, a project of the Southern Poverty Law Center, via Lindberg, 2017.)
https://www.tolerance.org/magazine/tell-transgender-students-were-still-here-for-you

Resources for Trans Youth

TYEF (Trans Youth Equality Foundation)
http://www.transyouthequality.org

TYEF (Trans Youth Equality Foundation)
http://www.transyouthequality.org/binders (features binder-specific information and video)

Point of Pride
https://pointofpride.org/chest-binder-donations
Provides free chest binders for any trans person who needs one but cannot afford or safely obtain one

GLAAD (formerly the Gay and Lesbian Alliance Against Defamation) is an American nongovernmental media monitoring organization founded by LGBT people in the media.
https://www.glaad.org

***Mary's Monster: Love, Madness, and How Mary Shelley Created Frankenstein* by Lita Judge**
Roaring Book Press
January 30, 2018
ISBN: 978-1626725003

Grades: 7 and up

Content Tags:
adultery, astronomy, death, family dynamics, first love/sex, French Revolution, ghoulish, mental illness, misogyny, outcast, scandal, suicidal ideation, suicide, survival, teen pregnancy/teen mothers

Summary

Many recognize Mary Shelley's name as the author of *Frankenstein*. However, what most people don't know is that before the age of twenty, she had already been disowned by her family and was living with a married man in a scandalous arrangement. She survived losing two babies just after their births, before pouring her anguish into the book that was first published anonymously. Years later, Lord Byron made public letters proving that Mary Shelley was in fact the anonymous author of *Frankenstein*. Free verse is paired with haunting black-and-white watercolor illustrations in this unique biography in verse.

Mental Health Poetry Activity

Mental illness is clearly a theme throughout *Mary's Monster*. Did you know that one in five people will suffer from a mental health issue at some point during their lifetime? That means some of your friends and family—including you—may be struggling with one right now. Read the action guide given here for facts about mental health and to learn how you can use poetry to address mental health in your life and community.

How. Mental illness affects the way a person's brain works and how they react to certain events. Sometimes people are born with a mental illness, like bipolar disorder. Other times, certain events like being bullied at school or overall stress can trigger a mental illness. This can result in an eating disorder, depression, or suicidal thoughts, for example.

Who. Some people who have a high risk of developing a mental health problem have low self-esteem or hate the way they look. Other people at risk include GLBTQ teens who are often bullied for their sexual orientation, or teens or do not have a stable support system like family or close friends. Experiencing a big life change—like moving to a new country, losing a parent or close friend, experiencing war or violence, or parents returning from war—can also put someone at risk for developing mental health problems.

Background. A person's race or class can impact how they are affected by a mental illness. For example, some people can't afford mental health care—even if they have insurance. In some communities, mental health problems carry a stigma that makes it more difficult for people to talk about their problems and seek help. Further still, it can be hard for people who don't speak English to find a provider who they can communicate with; for some immigrants, it's even more difficult to find a provider who understands their culture.

Know how to help. People who know someone with a mental health problem often do not take notice of the signs or are too late to help. You can help yourself and others by understanding the facts about mental health and knowing how to find help.

You are not alone. If you or someone you know is suffering from a mental illness, remember that you are NEVER alone. Talk to an adult—like a school counselor or health care provider—about finding help in your own community.

Poetry! What are your experiences with mental illness? Are you affected by the stigmas that surround it? One of the best ways to process these feelings to write about them with your poetry.

Inform. Now that you have the facts, it's time to inform others about mental illnesses. Why not start with poetry?

(Shared with permission from Wiener and PowerPoetry.org, 2019)

Remember that teens have the right to privacy and may not want to share their poetry, but rather use it for their own self-awareness and catharsis. This activity is meant to look within or to dig deep to think about ways to advocate for others with mental illness, not out anyone or make them uncomfortable in any way.

Because mental health can be such a personal subject, free verse is a recommended option for this activity.

Curriculum Connections

CCSS.ELA-LITERACY.CCRA.R.3 CCSS.ELA-LITERACY.CCRA.R.4
 CCSS.ELA-LITERACY.CCRA.R.6
CCSS.ELA-LITERACY.CCRA.W.1 CCSS.ELA-LITERACY.
 CCRA.W.2 CCSS.ELA-LITERACY.CCRA.W.3
CCSS.ELA-LITERACY.CCRA.W.4 CCSS.ELA-LITERACY.
 CCRA.W.7 CCSS.ELA-LITERACY.CCRA.W.9
AASL.I.A.2 AASL.I.B.3 AASL.II.B.2 AASL.II.B.3 AASL.IIIC.2 AASL.
 IV.A.1 AASL.IV.A.2
AASL.IV.A.3 AASL.IV.C.4 AASL.V.A.2 AASL.VI.2

Be sure to share the resources here with teens:
National Suicide Prevention Lifeline
www.suicidepreventionlifeline.org
If you are in crisis, please call this number right now, 24 hours a day, for help:
 800-273-8255.

NAMI (National Alliance on Mental Illness)

Call 800-950-6264 or visit https://www.nami.org

The largest grassroots mental health organization in the United States, it is dedicated to helping people affected by mental illness, and to obliterating the stigma associated with these diseases.

Strength of Us

www.strengthofus.org

An online community designed to inspire young adults affected by mental health issues to think positive, stay strong, and achieve their goals through peer support and resource sharing.

Free Clinics

www.freeclinics.com

If you are sick, this website will help you find free medical care, wherever you are.

Kiss of Broken Glass by Madeleine Kuderick
HarperTeen
September 9, 2014
ISBN: 978-0062306562

Grades: 9 and up

Content Tags:
cutting, depression, family dynamics, mental illness, self-harm, suicide, therapy

Summary

Fifteen-year-old Kenna is found cutting herself in the school bathroom, and she is sent to a psych ward for a 72-hour watch. One kiss of the blade was all it took to hook her back into cutting. When she meets other kids like her, will they be enough to make her forget cutting for a while?

Ekphrastic Poetry Activity

Ekphrasis is a Greek term meaning "description." Therefore, an ekphrastic poem is an expressive description of a scene, or more typically, a work of art. The poet can expand its meaning with vivid, eloquent reflections of the piece. In the book, Skylar writes an ekphrastic poem for Kenna that is based upon Kenna's own artwork, which they both find to be very powerful.

Use the following tips to guide writing an ekphrastic poem:

- Find a painting or sculpture that you find interesting. This could be a piece that you see in real life, or find a photo online.
- Look at the artwork, from different angles. Be mindful of how it makes you feel. Take notes about your thoughts and use multiple senses to help describe them.
- Who do you see in the painting/sculpture? What are they doing? What might they do afterward?
- Be creative with your poem! Try writing as if you were in the art, speaking to someone viewing it, or relating a conversation the people might have with each other. Imagine a story written about these people by the artist. Compare the art to something else, such as another statue or a busy day downtown. The possibilities are endless.

A painting to start with to discuss as an example could be *The Scream* by Edvard Munch (1893). The energy in this painting certainly gives viewers a lot to work with in creating powerful descriptions. To help teens with finding pieces of art to write about, try visiting https://www.metmuseum.org to choose from the massive, impressive collection of New York's Metropolitan Museum of Art.

Curriculum Connections

CCSS.ELA-LITERACY.CCRA.R.3 CCSS.ELA-LITERACY.CCRA.R.4
    CCSS.ELA-LITERACY.CCRA.R.6
CCSS.ELA-LITERACY.CCRA.W.1 CCSS.ELA-LITERACY.
    CCRA.W.2 CCSS.ELA-LITERACY.CCRA.W.3
CCSS.ELA-LITERACY.CCRA.W.4 CCSS.ELA-LITERACY.
    CCRA.W.7 CCSS.ELA-LITERACY.CCRA.W.9
AASL.I.A.2 AASL.I.B.3 AASL.II.A.2 AASL.IV.B.4 AASL.V.B.1 AASL.
    VI.C.2

Resources for Those Struggling with Self-harm:

S.A.F.E. Alternatives
Visit www.selfinjurycom or call the 800-DON'T-CUT (800-366-8288) referral line.
A nationally recognized treatment approach, professional network, and educational resource base that is committed to helping achieve an end to self-injurious behavior.

To Write Love on Her Arms
www.twloha.com
A nonprofit movement dedicated to presenting hope and finding help for
people struggling with addiction, depression, self-injury, and suicide.

Recover Your Life
www.selfharm.net
One of the largest self-harm support communities online, welcoming and supporting those who struggle with self-harm and other issues such as eating
disorders, mental health issues, and abuse.

National Suicide Hotline
800-SUICIDE (800-784-2433)

Inside Out & Back Again by Thanhha Lai
HarperCollins
February 22, 2011
ISBN: 978-0061962783

Grades: 4–8

Content Tags:
baptism, Christian, communism, death, family dynamics, grief, immigrants,
Muslim, poverty, refugees, religion, Vietnamese, Vietnam War, war

Summary

Ha's father left for a navy mission nine years ago and was captured. Her
family have moved south to get farther away from communism and are living
in poverty. They flee to Guam and are then flown to another tent city in the
United States, living with a sponsor in Alabama. All the family members start
new schools and jobs and work on learning English. Ha has always been very
smart, but she doesn't feel smart now at school as she learns a new language.
This story mirrors the author's own experiences growing up, and things that
she has noticed in her own nieces and nephews. Grief and healing via family
are themes that resonate throughout the text.

Found Poetry Activity

Ha has always been smart, but learning a new language takes some time—
especially English, with all its complications. Found poetry is a terrific option
for English as a Second Language/English Language Learners (ESL/ELL) students and anyone that feels a bit intimidated coming up with the words for
their own poems. Found poetry is a type of poetry created by taking words,

phrases, and sometimes whole sentences from other sources and reframing them by altering the sequence, adding or deleting text, changing spacing, and other changes in order to construct new meaning. Think of found poetry as a collage of sorts, but with words instead of pictures.

Before meeting with teens, copy a short chapter or several pages from *Inside Out & Back Again* for each teen. This is fair use—it's okay to use this small amount for educational purposes, really! Give each person the handout and a highlight marker. Instruct each person to read through the material while highlighting certain passages that stood out to them. The passages could then be sequenced in various ways to create poetry that is found within the book. They can be cut out and mounted on index cards, or just numbered with a pen next to the highlighted passages to create a new sequence. This form is ideal for teens who claim they can't write poetry. Once they are introduced to found poetry, they may become more confident and interested in poetry in general. This activity can be repeated and changed with different books, of course.

Curriculum Connections

CCSS.ELA-LITERACY.CCRA.R.2 CCSS.ELA-LITERACY.CCRA.R.4
CCSS.ELA-LITERACY.CCRA.R.5
CCSS.ELA-LITERACY.CCRA.R.7 CCSS.ELA-LITERACY.CCRA.W.2
CCSS.ELA-LITERACY.CCRA.W.4
AASL.I.A.2 AASL.I.B.3 AASL II.D.2 AASL.IV.A.3 AASL.V.B.2

Up from the Sea by Leza Lowitz
Crown Books for Young Readers
January 12, 2016
ISBN: 978-0553534740

Grades: 8 and up

Content Tags:
biracial, death, family dynamics, foster care, grief, Japan, natural disasters, 9/11, soccer, tsunami

Summary

On one disastrous day in March 2011, Kai loses almost everyone and everything he cares about when a tsunami devastates his Japanese village. Later that year, he is offered a trip to New York City to meet kids whose lives were affected by 9/11, and he realizes that he has the chance to find his estranged

American father while there. On the tenth anniversary of the tragedy, Kai visits Ground Zero and decides the way to make something good come out of something bad is to return home and help rebuild his own town.

Although a work of fiction, the author was in Tokyo when the Great East Japan Earthquake and Tsunami hit off the Pacific coast of the country on March 11, 2011. Fortunately, from her relatively close but "safe" home, her family was all okay. Her idea of a boy who loves soccer was inspired by a boy she met in the disaster zone.

Haiku Activity

If you have a good ear for music, you've got a head start in writing haiku. But even if you're not a music fan, don't worry; it's easy to pick up the rhythm of this ancient form of Japanese poetry.

Haiku are short poems that don't rhyme, but instead focus on the total number of syllables in each line. Traditional haiku use a total of 17 syllables spread over three lines of text. Most haiku use a formula of 5-7-5: The first and third lines contain 5 syllables and the middle line contains 7. (Some modern haiku use variations on this formula.)

HAIKU-WRITING TIPS

Choose a topic. Nature is the traditional source of inspiration for haiku, but no topics are off limits. What is something that you know or care a lot about? For example, you can write about your pet, your garage band, or your favorite piece of clothing. Get creative!

Consider the message you'd like to deliver. Why write the poem? What's especially interesting about your topic? Try to think of a twist or an unexpected connection for your reader to consider. For instance, you could write about how your basketball team suffered a terrible losing streak of twenty-five games in a row, but then turned things around, made the playoffs, and won the championship.

Follow the formula. Put some words on the page and count the syllables on each line. Change them around until they match the 5-7-5 syllable structure. Reading your words aloud may help you find the right rhythm.

Use a thesaurus. This tool helps you find synonyms (words that have the same definitions as other words) that will allow you to reach your 5-7-5 syllable count. For instance, the word "nice" has one syllable, "friendly" has two syllables, "sociable" has three syllables, and "personable" has four syllables, but all those words can be used interchangeably.

> ***Center it.*** Once your haiku is complete, center the text on the page (as opposed to aligning it on the left, as you would for an English paper). That's the traditional way of presenting a haiku.
>
> (Shared with permission from Wiener and PowerPoetry.org, 2019)

Curriculum Connections

CCSS.ELA-LITERACY.CCRA.R.2 CCSS.ELA-LITERACY.CCRA.R.4
   CCSS.ELA-LITERACY.CCRA.R.6
CCSS.ELA-LITERACY.CCRA.R.7 CCSS.ELA-LITERACY.CCRA.W.1
   CCSS.ELA-LITERACY.CCRA.W.2
CCSS.ELA-LITERACY.CCRA.W.4 AASL.I.A.2 AASL.I.B.3 AASL.
   II.A.2 AASL.IV.B.4 AASL.V.B.1
AASL.VI.C.2

***Under the Mesquite* by Guadalupe Garcia McCall**
Lee and Low Books
September 9, 2011
ISBN: 978-1600604294

Grades: 7 and up

Content Tags:
body image, cancer, Catholicism, college, death, family dynamics, grief, Mexican American, performing arts, poverty, resilience, serious illness, surgery

Summary

As the oldest of eight children of Mexican American immigrants, Lupita is forced to grow up fast when Mami is diagnosed with cancer. During the course of illness, poverty, death, and grief, Lupita emerges resilient and determined.

No one goes through life without experiencing loss. Grieving for a relative, friend, or schoolmate who has passed away can be one of life's toughest challenges. Loss can also come in other forms, like moving house, being injured, or finding out that somebody isn't trustworthy. All these things can affect us deeply, and sometimes it can feel pretty overwhelming.

If like the protagonist, Lupita, you've suffered a great loss like the death of someone close to you, reading or writing poetry that reflects on this painful experience can ease your pain. Believe it or not, reading or writing poetry that reflects on dark times can actually give you a sense of comfort and help you to work through what you're feeling (or to better understand what friends may be going through). Many writers use poetry to express feelings of loss.

R.I.P. Poems: How to Write a Poem About Death

As it is inevitable for us all, death is a universal experience that affects every single person. Dealing with such intense pain can be hard to manage, and to write about the death of a loved one or friend is hard. It is a theme that tugs at our deepest, most naked human emotions. While no words can do justice to a life that is lost, poetry is a tool that can help you process the loss and is extremely effective as a coping mechanism during difficult times of mourning or grief. It is an avenue of self-expression in which all your pain, loss, and suffering takes written form, and the completed product is one of severity and truth. This tip guide will further assist you in writing poetry about death and grief while mourning.

Take your time. The topic of death is very heavy. It requires utmost vulnerability and vitality in language. You may not be ready to approach writing about the recent injury to your soul right away, and that is perfectly fine. Breathe. We all grieve in our own ways. Take your time to process as you see appropriate. As the poet John Donne wrote, "Death be not proud." Take necessary measures, alone or with others, before attempting to organize your thoughts.

Withhold nothing. When you are ready to start writing, bring everything to the foreground. Hold nothing back. This step is a great time to go all out in writing what is on your mind. Let it out. It may be hard, but after some time, you will be comfortable with the truths you are putting on paper. Do not be afraid of your emotions or your memories, whether good or bad. This poem is yours and needs no validation from anyone else. You own yourself, and you own your work. Your words will carry the weight you feel during your time of mourning. Refuse nothing from your pen as it becomes transfixed to your thoughts.

Have a powerful, poetic purpose. What is the purpose of this poem? What are you trying to accomplish or clarify? Are you sharing an anecdote? Saying something specific to the person you've lost? Maybe this is your last goodbye? It is important that you refer to your initial outpouring of words to determine a general theme in your creative output. Observe the underlying messages, as this will help you develop ideas for imagery and format when you write your poem. Consult the "Glossary of Poetic Devices" in the back of the book for new techniques.

Compose yourself—and your poem. Take your revisions and analysis from the earlier stages in your creative process and compose your poem. Reflect on the sentimental value that the person had to you. Bring those feelings to your poem. It will add flavor and uniqueness to the poem that will make it forever stand out. This process of writing will further help you work through the mourning process.

Don't be afraid to share. Your poetry can help you find the light after the darkness that death and grief bring. Your words also have the power to inspire others to enjoy the beauty of life. Emily Dickinson wrote, "A Death blow is a Life blow to some / Who till they died, did not alive become." Your poem can speak life into someone who may be struggling or help someone live life to the fullest. If you believe your poem is more intimate or suitable for a select audience, feel free to keep that for your own. But if there is room for sharing, use your experiences and strength and give it to the world. You have a community of poets that will benefit from reading your words. Writing about the tragedy will ultimately help you to heal and grow stronger.

(Shared with permission from Wiener and PowerPoetry.org)
As always, privacy is permitted for those who want it.

Curriculum Connections

CCSS.ELA-LITERACY.CCRA.R.3 CCSS.ELA-LITERACY.CCRA.R.4
    CCSS.ELA-LITERACY.CCRA.R.6
CCSS.ELA-LITERACY.CCRA.W.3 CCSS.ELA-LITERACY.
    CCRA.W.4 CCSS.ELA-LITERACY.CCRA.W.10
AASL.I.A.2 AASL.I.B.3 AASL.II.B.2 AASL.II.B.3 AASL.IIIC.2 AASL.
    IV.A.1 AASL.IV.A.2
AASL.IV.A.3 AASL.IV.C.4 AASL.V.A.2 AASL.VI.2

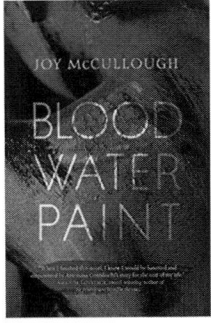

***Blood Water Paint* by Joy McCullough**
Dutton Books for Young Readers
March 6, 2018
ISBN: 978-0735232112

Grades: 8 and up

Content Tags:
art history, misogyny, painting, parables, sexual assault/abuse

Summary

After her mother passes away when Artemisia is only twelve, she has two choices: become a nun in a convent or work for her father grinding pigment for his paint. She chooses the latter, and painting becomes her life. Surrounded by misogyny and sexual abuse, Artemisia is one of the most talented painters of the time, but no one knows her name. The biblical parables of Judith and Susannah are interspersed in this hybrid of prose and verse.

Ekphrastic Poetry Activity

Ekphrasis is a Greek term meaning "description." Therefore, an ekphrastic poem is an expressive description of a scene, or more typically, a work of art. The poet can expand its meaning with vivid, eloquent reflections of the piece. Artemisia Gentileschi used her paintings as visual descriptions. Provide several images of Artemisia's paintings for teens to choose from.

Note: Some of these paintings involve partial nudity, so if that is a concern, choose carefully.

Use the following tips to guide writing an ekphrastic poem:

- Find a painting or sculpture that you find interesting. This could be a piece that you see in real life, or find a photo online.

- Look at the artwork, from different angles. Be mindful of how it makes you feel. Take notes about your thoughts and use multiple senses to help describe them.

- Who do you see in the painting/sculpture? What are they doing? What might they do afterward?

- Be creative with your poem! Try writing as if you were in the art, speaking to someone viewing it, or relating a conversation the people might have with each other. Imagine a story written about these people by the artist. Compare the art to something else, such as another statue or a busy day downtown. The possibilities are endless.

Curriculum Connections

CCSS.ELA-LITERACY.CCRA.R.2 CCSS.ELA-LITERACY.CCRA.R.4
   CCSS.ELA-LITERACY.CCRA.R.6
CCSS.ELA-LITERACY.CCRA.R.7 CCSS.ELA-LITERACY.CCRA.W.1
   CCSS.ELA-LITERACY.CCRA.W.2
CCSS.ELA-LITERACY.CCRA.W.4 AASL.I.A.2 AASL.I.B.3 AASL.
   II.A.2 AASL.IV.B.4
AASL.V.B.1 AASL.VI.C.2

Joy McCullough would like survivors to know they are not alone.

Resources for Survivors of Sexual Violence

National Sexual Violence Resource Center
www.nsvrc.org

RAINN (Rape, Abuse, and Incest National Network)
Visit www.rainn.org or call 800-656-HOPE (4673) for confidential trained
  assistance

What I Leave Behind by Alison McGhee
Atheneum/Caitlyn Dlouhy Books
May 15, 2018
ISBN: 978-1481476560

Grades: 8 and up

Content Tags:
Black, Bowie, David, grief, homelessness, Latinx,
sexual assault/abuse, suicide, therapy

Summary

After his father commits suicide, Will begins walking . . . and walking . . .
and walking. But walking doesn't take away his urge to re-create his dad's famous
cornbread recipe, which he just can't seem to get right. When he learns that his
friend Playa has been raped at a party, he decides to do some good in the world
to avoid his own sadness. He begins leaving small gifts for people in his life, from
the homeless guy "Superman," to a neighborhood kid known as "Little Butterfly
Dude," to his dear friend, Playa. By helping others, he begins to move past his
own trauma. This novel in verse is told in 100 poems of 100 words each.

Penny Poetry Activity

Alison McGhee's poems in this book are brief but mighty. Adding one
deliberate word at a time, she doles them out like pennies until she gets to 100
on each page. The number 100 has significance in multiple ways in this story:
there are exactly 100 poems of exactly 100 words each, and one dollar (100
pennies) is the cost of each item that Will buys to give others. This activity is
open ended, in that it is free verse, but specific in that penny poems must be
100 words each. Advise students to choose wisely and to use a thesaurus to
substitute words or phrases as needed so they reach *exactly* 100—99 won't do
it, and neither will 101. No change will be given, so don't go over one dollar!

Curriculum Connections

CCSS.ELA-LITERACY.CCRA.R.2 CCSS.ELA-LITERACY.CCRA.R.4
  CCSS.ELA-LITERACY.CCRA.R.6
CCSS.ELA-LITERACY.CCRA.R.7 CCSS.ELA-LITERACY.CCRA.W.1
  CCSS.ELA-LITERACY.CCRA.W.2
CCSS.ELA-LITERACY.CCRA.W.4 AASL.I.A.2 AASL.I.B.3 AASL.
  III.C.2 AASL.IV.B.4 AASL.V.B.1

Alison McGhee would like readers struggling with feelings of hopeless and despair to know they are not alone.

Here are good resources that can help:

- For depression or thoughts of suicide, call 800-273-TALK (8255) or text NAMI to 741-741 for help.
- Anyone who is sexually assaulted should call 800-656-4673 or visit RAINN .org for help.

Amiri & Odette: A Love Story by Walter Dean Myers
Paintings by Javaka Steptoe
Scholastic Press
January 1, 2009
ISBN: 978-0590680417

Grades: 7 and up

Content Tags:
basketball, Black, dance, first love/sex, gang violence, poverty

Summary

With the gorgeous mixed-media artwork of Javaka Steptoe and his signature lyrical voice, Walter Dean Myers creates a modern retelling of the ballet *Swan Lake,* surrounded by poverty, basketball, and gang violence.

Swan Lake Sonnet Activity

The vibrant illustrations and text that varies in size, color, boldness, and case help convey the sentiments throughout *Amiri & Odette.* Music from *Swan Lake* also has the ability to prompt emotions and mood. Given here are two scannable QR codes connected to videos of the traditional Tchaikovsky version of *Swan Lake* music, and then an urban mix version of *Swan Lake*. (Note: There is an explicit language advisory on the urban mix version.)

Play both versions for teens, having them write down words and phrases that come to mind from each one. Next, they select one of the versions to use as inspiration for a sonnet. A sonnet can be a perfect style of poetry for expressing strong emotions. There are varied types of sonnets, so for this activity, use the following format. Sonnets are fourteen-line poems with a variable rhyme scheme. There must be three sets of four lines, followed by one set of two lines. The sets of four lines are called quatrains, and the last set of two lines is a couplet. The rhyme scheme is as follows:

First quatrain: ABAB

Second quatrain: CDCD

Third quatrain: EFEF

Couplet: GG

Simonov and London Philharmonic Orchestra (2012), Tchaikovsky—*Swan Lake* (Swan Theme), posted May 21.
https://www.youtube.com/watch?v=9cNQFB0TDfY

Meany—Swan Lake urban mix, posted February 5, 2009.
https://www.youtube.com/watch?v=d6UfySXJ6K0

Curriculum Connections

CCSS.ELA-LITERACY.CCRA.R.2 CCSS.ELA-LITERACY.CCRA.R.4
   CCSS.ELA-LITERACY.CCRA.R.6
CCSS.ELA-LITERACY.CCRA.R.7 CCSS.ELA-LITERACY.CCRA.W.1
   CCSS.ELA-LITERACY.CCRA.W.2
CCSS.ELA-LITERACY.CCRA.W.4 CCSS.ELA-LITERACY.
   CCRA.W.8 AASL.I.A.2 AASL.I.B.3
AASL.II.A.2 AASL.IV.B.4 AASL.V.B.1 AASL.VI.C.2

Street Love by Walter Dean Myers
Amistad
October 30, 2007
ISBN: 978-0064407328

Grades: 8 and up

Content Tags:
Black, classism, family dynamics, first love/sex, foster care, Harlem, incarceration, poverty, racism, survival

Summary

Damien's mother thinks that his first love, Junice, is not worthy and totally wrong for him. Junice is fighting to survive and meet the needs of her little sister, in the face of her mother with two felonies and facing possible foster care. Sharon Draper, an award-winning author of many middle-grade and YA books, blurbs this book as a "Harlem-esque *Romeo and Juliet*."

Point-of-View Cinquain Activity

Point of view encompasses the way that a story is narrated or portrayed and who is telling the story. The point of view shapes the perception from a particular angle as the story unfolds. This can in turn influence its tone and can be a strong factor in manipulating the reader's understanding of the narrative.

The two most common point-of-view approaches are the first person, where the story is told by the narrator from their perspective. The other is third person, where the narrator is separate from the events of the story and tells the story using all third-person pronouns or proper nouns for all characters and places presented.

Cinquain poems are similar to other Japanese poetic forms like haiku and tanka. They are five lines long, with a syllable pattern of 2, 4, 6, 8, 2. They sometimes rhyme, but usually do not.

A didactic cinquain is a specific kind of cinquain, which follows the pattern given here:

Line 1: One word, usually a noun, which also serves as the title of the poem

Line 2: Two adjectives describing the title.

Line 3: Three verbs that show action.

Line 4: A short sentence that show emotions about the poem's subject.

Line 5: A one-word synonym of the title.

Have teens choose two different points of view from any two characters in *Street Love*, and using the criteria for didactic cinquains, write two of them, one representing each point of view selected. This activity translates well to spoken word poetry, with teens reading the different point-of-view cinquains as if two people are having a conversation.

Curriculum Connections

CCSS.ELA-LITERACY.CCRA.R.2 CCSS.ELA-LITERACY.CCRA.R.4
    CCSS.ELA-LITERACY.CCRA.R.6
CCSS.ELA-LITERACY.CCRA.R.7 CCSS.ELA-LITERACY.CCRA.W.1
    CCSS.ELA-LITERACY.CCRA.W.2
CCSS.ELA-LITERACY.CCRA.W.4 AASL.I.A.2 AASL.I.B.3 AASL.
    II.A.2 AASL.IV.B.4 AASL.V.B.1
AASL.VI.C.2

American Ace by Marilyn Nelson
Dial Books
January 12, 2016
ISBN: 978-0803733053

Grades: 7 and up

Content Tags:
Black, depression, DNA/ancestry, family dynamics, grief, HBCU, Irish, Italian, racial identity, Tuskegee Airmen

Summary

After Connor's grandmother dies, a letter is found with a confession that shakes up their close Italian American family. Connor's grandfather, the man who raised his father, is not actually the birth father. When the only clues to the identity of this man are a pair of pilot's wings and a class ring, Connor decides to investigate himself. What he discovers will change the understanding of identity and race within their entire family.

Scan this QR code for a brief biography of these history makers, "Tuskegee Airmen; A Short Biography" (Digital Video Technology Suncoast Technical College 2015). https://www.youtube.com/watch?v=bcFEwgoWymo.

Identity Poetry Activity

Connor discovers that his biological grandfather was actually a Tuskegee Airman.

Nelson's poem "Beyond Skin" on page 117 in *American Ace* takes on identity and what it means to each of us:

> I feel like there's a blackness beyond skin,
> beyond race, beyond outward appearance.
> A blackness that has more to do with how
> You see than how you're seen. That craves justice
> equally for oneself and for others.
> I hope I've found some of that in myself.

What does it mean to be a descendant of a Tuskegee Airman? What is Nelson trying to say in "Beyond Skin"? Identity can encompass a variety of designations for a single person. I may see myself as librarian, daughter, sister, friend, White, short, blonde, smart, Irish, and Hungarian. Someone else may see my identity a different way, depending on whose point of view it is, or in what context they know me (or don't know me).

Encourage teens to think about what they know about their own identities. Do pieces from your past affect who you are today? Teens write poems in free verse about their own identities. This could be the identity they feel themselves, or how they think that others perceive their identities. Privacy is permitted, and volunteers may share their verse with the group.

Curriculum Connections

CCSS.ELA-LITERACY.CCRA.R.1 CCSS.ELA-LITERACY.CCRA.R.2
CCSS.ELA-LITERACY.CCRA.R.3
CCSS.ELA-LITERACY.CCRA.R.4 CCSS.ELA-LITERACY.CCRA.R.6
CCSS.ELA-LITERACY.CCRA.W.3
CCSS.ELA-LITERACY.CCRA.W.4 AASL.I.A.2 AASL.I.D.3 AASL.
II.A.2 AASL.II.B.3
AASL. II. D.3 AASL.III.C.2 AASL.IV.B.2 AASL.V.B.1
AASL.VI.C.2

***How I Discovered Poetry* by Marilyn Nelson**
Dial Books
January 14, 2014
ISBN: 978-0803733046

Grades: 6 and up

Content Tags:
Black, church, Civil Rights Era/Movement, geeks, military, moving, racial identity, racism, segregation, self-awareness, teachers, writing

Summary

Nelson's Civil Rights era memoir in verse unfolds through poems of her growing awareness and worldview regarding racial tensions, feminism, and the Cold War.

Open Sonnet Activity

Nelson states in her author's note that she wrote this book in a sequence of fifty unrhymed sonnets. A sonnet can be a perfect style of poetry for expressing emotions. Sonnets are fourteen-line poems with a variable rhyme scheme. She has chosen to use the traditional fourteen-line length with a rough approximation of iambic pentameter (ten syllables per line, with every other word stressed).

For this activity, have teens follow the form that Nelson uses. Topics can be anything from the book that they connect with (for ideas, see the content tags, although teens are not limited to just these). For additional challenge, add in some poetic devices from the glossary in the back of this book.

Curriculum Connections

CCSS.ELA-LITERACY.CCRA.R.2 CCSS.ELA-LITERACY.CCRA.R.4
   CCSS.ELA-LITERACY.CCRA.R.6
CCSS.ELA-LITERACY.CCRA.R.7 CCSS.ELA-LITERACY.CCRA.W.1
   CCSS.ELA-LITERACY.CCRA.W.2
CCSS.ELA-LITERACY.CCRA.W.4 AASL.I.A.2 AASL.I.B.3 AASL.
   II.A.2 AASL.IV.B.4 AASL.V.B.1
AASL.VI.C.2

***Loving vs. Virginia: A Documentary Novel
of the Landmark Civil Rights Case***
**by Patricia Hruby Powell
Artwork by Shadra Strickland
Chronicle Books
January 31, 2017
ISBN: 978-1452125909**

Grades: 8 and up

Content Tags:
Civil Rights Era/Movement, interracial marriage, jail, prejudice, racism, segregation

Summary

This fictionalized historical documentary in verse depicts an interracial couple who fell in love and married. During a time of segregation, injustices, and prejudice, Richard and Mildred Loving were the focus of a landmark civil rights case that legalized marriage between races.

Protest Poetry Activity

Richard and Mildred Loving had a name that was prophetic. They just wanted to love each other and be married and raise a family together. Unfortunately, racist segregationalist laws at the time kept getting in their way. They continued the protest, fighting to love who they wanted, and won in the end after many years of standing up for what is right. Just as the Lovings stood up for what they believed in, teens can too, by using poetry to express themselves.

> Pithy and powerful, poetry is a popular art form at protests and rallies. From the civil rights and women's liberation movements to Black Lives Matter, poetry is commanding enough to gather crowds in a city square and compact enough to demand attention on social media. Speaking truth to power remains a crucial role of the poet in the face of political and media rhetoric designed to obscure, manipulate, or worse . . . poetry is necessary and sought after in moments of political crisis. (Poetry Foundation 2019)

Teens may want to protest a variety of current policies and events. One way to protest peacefully is by writing to fight as part of activism. Writing poetry can be a way of using our voices and can provide a sense of empowerment during challenging times (Salfia 2018).

When we write to fight, we are using our voices against racism, sexism, and xenophobia. Whatever your cause may be: write to fight. Musicians write to fight all the time. Bob Dylan's musical protests became anthems of sorts during the Civil Rights Movement, while modern performers like Kendrick Lamar rap about politics in the hood.

Teens will write a persuasive protest poem about a topic of their choosing. For more resources to accompany this activity, see *Fight the Power: Music as a Social Force,* written by the author of this book for *School Library Journal's Teen Librarian Toolbox, 2019.* http://www.teenlibrariantoolbox.com/2019/02/fight -the-power-music-as-a-social-force-a-guest-post-by-lisa-krok.

Curriculum Connections

CCSS.ELA-LITERACY.CCRA.R.3 CCSS.ELA-LITERACY.CCRA.R.4
CCSS.ELA-LITERACY.CCRA.R.6

CCSS.ELA-LITERACY.CCRA.R.7 CCSS.ELA-LITERACY.CCRA.W.1
CCSS.ELA-LITERACY.CCRA.W.2
CCSS.ELA-LITERACY.CCRA.W.3 CCSS.ELA-LITERACY.
CCRA.W.4 CCSS.ELA-LITERACY.CCRA.W.7
CCSS.ELA-LITERACY.CCRA.W.8 CCSS.ELA-LITERACY.
CCRA.W.9 AASL.I.A.2 AASL.I.B.3
AASL.I.D.1 AASL.I.D.3 AASL.II.B.2 AASL.II.C.2 AASL.III.C.2
AASL.III.D.2 AASL.IV.D.2
AASL.V.A.2 AASL.V.B.1 AASL.V.C.1 AASL.VI.C.2

Gabi, a Girl in Pieces by Isabel Quintero
Artwork by Zeke Peña
Cinco Puntos Press
October 14, 2014
ISBN: 978-1935955948

Grades: 9 and up

Content Tags:
abortion, addiction, body image, college applications, death, domestic violence, first love/sex, Latinx, LGBTQ+, overdose, prom, religion, self-harm, sexual assault/abuse, teen pregnancy/teen mothers

Summary

Gabi Hernandez reports her last year of high school in her diary through a hybrid of prose and verse, with a little bit of epistolary mixed in via letters. Named after her grandmother, who beat her mother upon discovering she was pregnant, Gabi navigates her own identity along with applying for college, her father's meth habit, body image issues, cute boys, and poetry.

Prose-to-Poetry Activity

Isabel Quintero uses a blend of literary forms throughout this book. Most notably, she goes back and forth from prose to verse. Why would an author do this? Think about how the meaning can alter, based upon different forms and points of view used. Browse through *Gabi, a Girl in Pieces* and select a page of prose or a prose passage. Try using a visual format when converting the prose to poetry. Some ideas are haiku, concrete, diamante, and sonnet. As always, remember that the thesaurus is your friend to help find alternative words to fit your poetry.

Haiku are short poems that don't rhyme, but instead focus on the total number of syllables in each line. Traditional haiku use a total of 17 syllables spread over three lines of text. Most haiku use a formula of 5-7-5: The first and third lines contain 5 syllables and the middle line contains 7 (Power Poetry.org, 2019).

Concrete poetry, also called *visual* or *shape poetry*, was created as a way to combine image and poetry. The importance of language is emphasized in this type of art, as the shapes the words make are just as important as what they say (Wiener and PowerPoetry.org, 2019).

A diamante is a poem of seven lines that does not rhyme. The first and last lines are the shortest, while the lines in the middle are longer, and the lines are centered, which gives diamante poems a diamond shape. Because *diamante* is the Italian word for *diamond*, these poems are named for their rhombus shape.

Kenn Nesbitt (2011) advises the following rules for diamantes:

> Diamantes are seven lines long.
>
> The first and last lines have just one word.
>
> The second and sixth lines have two words.
>
> The third and fifth lines have three words.
>
> And the fourth line has four words.
>
> Lines 1, 4, and 7 have nouns.
>
> Lines 2 and 6 have adjectives.
>
> Lines 3 and 5 have verbs.

Here's an easy way to visualize all three rules:

Noun

Adj., Adj.

Verb, Verb, Verb

Noun, Noun, Noun, Noun

Verb, Verb, Verb

Adj., Adj.

Noun

There are two types of these poems: synonym and antonym diamantes. In a synonym diamante, the nouns in the first and last lines mean basically the same thing. In an antonym diamante, the nouns in the first and last lines are opposites. Also, centering your poem in the middle of the page helps make the diamond shape more apparent.

A sonnet can be a perfect style of poetry for expressing strong emotions. There are varied types of sonnets, so for this activity, use the following format. Sonnets are fourteen-line poems with a variable rhyme scheme. There must be three sets of four lines, followed by one set of two lines. The sets of four lines are called quatrains, and the last set of two lines is a couplet. The rhyme scheme is as follows:

First quatrain: ABAB

Second quatrain: CDCD

Third quatrain: EFEF

Couplet: GG

Does the new version seem to reflect the words a bit differently? How? When finished, try the reverse—choose a poem from the book and re-create it as prose. Pay special attention to line breaks and pacing. Did it change the meaning? Was it more or less powerful? Which format did you prefer?

Curriculum Connections

CCSS.ELA-LITERACY.CCRA.R.2 CCSS.ELA-LITERACY.CCRA.R.4 CCSS.ELA-LITERACY.CCRA.R.6
CCSS.ELA-LITERACY.CCRA.R.7 CCSS.ELA-LITERACY.CCRA.W.1 CCSS.ELA-LITERACY.CCRA.W.2
CCSS.ELA-LITERACY.CCRA.W.4 AASL.I.A.2 AASL.I.B.3 AASL.II.A.2 AASL.IV.B.4 AASL.V.B.1
AASL.VI.C.2

***For Every One* by Jason Reynolds**
Atheneum/Caitlyn Dlouhy Books
April 10, 2018
ISBN: 978-1481486248

Grades: 7 and up

Content Tags:
Black, courage, dreams, drive to succeed, passion

Summary

Jason Reynolds is a self-professed dreamer. He has been working to make his own dreams come true, but they take time . . . not just for Jason, but *For Every One*. Kids who may be scared to dream, or don't even try because they have never seen one of their dreams come true: Jason wants you to know that just having the dream is the spark you need; take a leap of faith from there.

Dream Poetry Activity

Poet Langston Hughes was also a dreamer. First, share his poem *Dreams* (1926), https://poets.org/poem/dreams. Encourage teens to explain what they think the poem means.

Next, share Hughes's poem *Harlem* (1951), https://www.poetryfoundation .org/poems/46548/harlem.

Encourage discussions debating the differences between these two poems and the messages and moods that each conveys.

Reynolds narrates the audio version of this book himself. Play that for the group to listen to while they are writing their own dream poems. Because dreams are personal and very open ended, teens select their form of choice for this activity. This can also evolve into spoken word poetry for those who are inclined. Additionally, *For Every One* and the Hughes poems are also valuable content to include when examining Dr. Martin Luther King, Jr.'s "I Have a Dream" speech.

Curriculum Connections

CCSS.ELA-LITERACY.CCRA.R.1 CCSS.ELA-LITERACY.CCRA.R.2
   CCSS.ELA-LITERACY.CCRA.R.3
CCSS.ELA-LITERACY.CCRA.R.4 CCSS.ELA-LITERACY.CCRA.R.6
   CCSS.ELA-LITERACY.CCRA.R.9
CCSS.ELA-LITERACY.CCRA.W.2 CCSS.ELA-LITERACY.
   CCRA.W.3 CCSS.ELA-LITERACY.CCRA.W.4
CCSS.ELA-LITERACY.CCRA.W.8 AASL.I.A.1 AASL.B.3 AASL.I.C.1
   AASL.I.D.3 AASL.II.A.2
AASL.II.B.2 AASL.II.B AASL.II.D.2 AASL.III.C.2 AASL.IV.B.2
   AASL.IV.B.4 AASL.IV.D.2
AASL.V.A.2 AASL.V.B.1 AASL.VI.D.2

Long Way Down **by Jason Reynolds**
Atheneum/Caitlyn Dlouhy Books
October 17, 2017
ISBN: 978-1481438254

Grades: 7 and up

Content Tags:
Black, death, decision-making, gun violence, revenge

Summary

After Will's brother Shawn is shot and killed, Will knows what he is expected to do. The rules are simple: no crying, no snitching, get revenge. With a piece shoved into the back of his jeans, he steps into the elevator. As the elevator doors open at each floor, Will is greeted by ghosts of sorts from his past who challenge his thoughts. Are seven floors and sixty seconds enough time for him to decide what to do?

Sixty-Second Poem Activity

Long Way Down takes place over the course of sixty seconds. When Will steps off the elevator onto the first floor, readers don't know his decision. Will he seek revenge as planned, or did his long way down with the visitors in the elevator change his mind? Armed with pencils, paper, and a stopwatch or timer (most phones have them), write your own ending to *Long Way Down* in just sixty seconds! When time is up, flip your paper over and write a different ending in just sixty seconds. This can also be done in seven sections of sixty-second intervals, to represent the seven floors as Will descends in the elevator. Be creative—this ending could take many paths. Have volunteers share their efforts aloud.

Curriculum Connections

CCSS.ELA-LITERACY.CCRA.R.1 CCSS.ELA-LITERACY.CCRA.R.4
    CCSS.ELA-LITERACY.CCRA.R.6
CCSS.ELA-LITERACY.CCRA.W.3 CCSS.ELA-LITERACY.
    CCRA.W.4 CCSS.ELA-LITERACY.CCRA.W.9
AASL.I.A.2 AASL.I.B.2 AASL.I.C.4 AASL.II.A.2 AASL.II.B.3 AASL.
    II.C.2 AASL.II.D2
AASL.III.A.2 AASL.III.B.2 AASL.III.C.2 AASL.IV.D.1 AASL.IV.B.2
    AASL. IV.B.3 AASL.IV.C.3
AASL. V.B.1 AASL.VI.C.2

Anagram Poetry Activity

An anagram is a play on words that is created by rearranging the letters of the original word to make a new word or phrase. Anagrams can be quite witty, often ending in hilarious results. Fun fact: a poet that specializes in anagrams is an anagrammarian. Will has a penchant for anagrams.

Anagrams can often be found in everyday life, such as in crossword puzzles, word scrambles, and word games like Boggle. Anagrams have intergenerational appeal. Kids, parents, and grandparents can enjoy solving the crossword puzzle or rearranging the letters in words and phrases to create new anagrams. Often, anagrams come from simple words with the letters scrambled to form new, random words that aren't usually connected.

Some examples of these are:

arc = car
elbow = below
dusty = study
stressed = desserts

A more challenging way to use anagrams is to create a connection to the original word or phrase:

listen = silent
astronomer = moon starer

Authors sometimes construct anagrams as a disguise of sorts for characters. Probably the most famous of these is J. K. Rowling's use:

Tom Marvolo Riddle = I am Lord Voldemort

Anagrams have also been created out of an artist's name, sometimes by the person themselves, creating an alter ego:

Jim Morrison = Mr. Mojo Risin'

Anagrams can also be created out of location names:

Paris = Pairs
Denver = Nerved
San Diego = Diagnose

Start simple with unrelated, single-word anagrams, then progress to the more challenging types. Writing together in pairs works well for this activity.

Curriculum Connections

CCSS.ELA-LITERACY.CCRA.R.4 CCSS.ELA-LITERACY.CCRA.W.4
    AASL.I.A.2
AASL.I.B.3 AASL.III.B.2 AASL.III.D.1 AASL.IV.B.4 AASL.IV.C.2
    AASL.V.B.1 AASL.VI.C.2

Girls Like Me by Lola StVil
HMH Books for Young Readers
October 4, 2016
ISBN: 978-0544706743

Grades: 7 and up

Content Tags:
blended family, body image, bullying, first love/sex, grief, LGBTQ+, self-esteem, serious illness, social media

Summary

Shay Summers is overweight, facing threats from a female bully at school, and coping with the death of her father. Insecure Shay begins falling for Blake, a mysterious boy online. She is afraid to tell him who she is, but her two best friends help her prevail.

Texting Couplets Activity

Sections of *Girls Like Me* include the texting interactions on Shay's phone. In poetry, a couplet is a pair of lines in a verse. Usually they rhyme, and they often share a rhythm as well. Together, they produce a complete thought.

Texting couplets are a fun way for teens to practice writing poetic couplets. Because text messaging is a language with which teens are very comfortable, this just takes it a step further, including rhyme and a pair that design a complete thought.

There are a few options of ways to do this. One way is obviously on actual phones, texting each other in couplet form. But not every student has a phone (believe it or not), so alternatives might be to write the couplets opposite each other in speech bubbles on a page, or using a computer to instant message or type up as a document. Depending on the particular needs of your class, using one or all three of these methods simultaneously may work best. Students could also be given their choice of methods, working in pairs. Encourage them to make it sound like a conversation between two friends.

Curriculum Connections

CCSS.ELA-LITERACY.CCRA.R.4 CCSS.ELA-LITERACY.CCRA.R.5
    CCSS.ELA-LITERACY.CCRA.W.3
CCSS.ELA-LITERACY.CCRA.W.4 AASL.I.A.2 AASL.I.B.3 AASL.
    II.A.2 AASL.IV.B.4 AASL.V.B.1
AASL.VI.C.2

The Moon Within by Aida Salazar
Arthur A. Levine Books
February 26, 2019
ISBN: 978-1338283372

Grades: 4–8

Content Tags:
Black, bomba, bullying, cultural traditions, dance, gender fluidity, gender identity, Indigenous, LGBTQ+, menstruation, puberty, Puerto Rican, Xicana

Summary

As Celi Rivera's body is changing, her mother is insisting on an ancestral ritual that Mima's community has reclaimed. Celi does *not* want to participate—she wants to take a stand. She is full of questions about her changing body, her best friend questioning being gender fluid, and her first attraction to a boy.

Bomba Poetry Activity

Celi has been participating in the Puerto Rican drum dance, bomba, since she was two years old. Bomba involves a connection and a challenge between a drummer and a dancer. The dancer presents a series of gestures, to which the drummer provides a synchronized beat. Therefore, it is the drummer who attempts to follow the dancer, and not the other way around, as takes place in other traditional dances. The dancer must be in very good shape physically, as the challenge will usually continue until either the dancer or the drummer stops first.

If you have a music department in your school with a drum you can borrow, do so. If you don't have access to a real drum, improvise by using any item that resonates with a sound similar to a drum. After watching the bomba video, have students with pencils ready as the beat begins. The leader beats the drum in a myriad of rhythms for 15 seconds or so at a time, as teens write free verse poetry coordinated

Scan this QR code for a video of bomba dancing in Puerto Rico. Pay special attention to how the drummer follows the dancer, adjusting his beat to her movements (Puerto Rican Bomba Dance—Sanse, 2017), https://www.youtube.com/watch?v=x3Gkta-3Jzw.

to that beat. Generally, faster beats will have more words of lesser syllables, while slower beats may induce verse having fewer words with more syllables. Try this first with the leader as the drummer, then given teens a chance to be the drummer while their friends write. Alternatively, download some bomba music and write that way, although the beats will change more frequently, creating more of a challenge when writing.

Curriculum Connections

CCSS.ELA-LITERACY.CCRA.R.7 CCSS.ELA-LITERACY.CCRA.R.9
    CCSS.ELA-LITERACY.CCRA.W.2
CCSS.ELA-LITERACY.CCRA.W.3 CCSS.ELA-LITERACY.
    CCRA.W.4 CCSS.ELA-LITERACY.CCRA.W.8
AASL.I.A.2 AASL.I.C.1 AASL.I. D.3 AASL.II.B.3 AASL.II.D.2 AASL.
    III.C.2 AASL.IV.B.1
AASL.IV.D.2 AASL.V.A.3 AASL.VI.C.2

The Opposite of Innocent by Sonya Sones
HarperTeen
September 4, 2018
ISBN: 978-0062370310

Grades: 7 and up

Content Tags:
older men, pedophilia, sexual assault/abuse

Summary

Lily was only twelve when a family friend, Luke, left for two years. Now that he is back, she feels transformed and can't wait to see Luke's reaction to seeing her. When he pays her special attention and kisses her, Lily thinks it is the real deal at first, even when her friends think anyone his age must be messed up to want to be with a fourteen-year-old. As things progress, Lily's eyes begin to open about Luke.

Concrete Poetry Activity

The teacher in this book assigned concrete poetry. Concrete poetry, also called *visual* or *shape poetry*, was created as a way to combine image and poetry. The importance of language is emphasized in this type of art, as the shapes the words make are just as important as what they say.

Write: With concrete poetry, it's a good idea to first write out your whole poem without putting it into a shape, and then let the words make up the shape later. There are no rules when it comes to a concrete poem, so you're free to let your imagination run wild and create any story you'd like! Don't worry about the length of your poem, but remember that the more words you have, the bigger your shape will be.

Shape: Pick a shape that you want your poem to create. If someone looks at your poem from far away, they will see the outline of the shape, but up close, they will actually be able to read the words. Knowing this, you will probably want to pick a pretty simple shape. First, think of what story your poem will tell, and match the shape to the theme of the poem. For example, if you are writing a love poem, you might want the poem to be shaped like a heart.

Draw: You don't need to be an artist to make this poem look great! Just draw an outline of the shape you picked, either on paper or with a drawing tool from a computer program like Paint (or Photoshop if you're feeling fancy). If you're going to draw your concrete poem by hand, you can always scan the picture and upload it to your computer so you have a virtual version too!

Words: Remember, the words of the poem are just as important as the shapes they make for a concrete poem. So, it's a good idea to experiment with using bold, italics, or even colors to add shade and texture to the words or to make whatever shape you use look three-dimensional! Then, either by hand or using a software program, paste the words of the poem you've written onto the outline of the shape in the order you want them to be read! Now, you will have created your own original poetic picture!

Make a Scene: Don't just stop at one shape—make a whole scene! Have fun writing a whole bunch of poems that are different lengths and turn them into all different sizes and shapes to create an image that tells its own story!

(Shared with permission from Wiener and PowerPoetry.org, 2019)

Curriculum Connections

CCSS.ELA-LITERACY.CCRA.R.7 CCSS.ELA-LITERACY.CCRA.R.9
    CCSS.ELA-LITERACY.CCRA.W.2
CCSS.ELA-LITERACY.CCRA.W.3 CCSS.ELA-LITERACY.
    CCRA.W.4 CCSS.ELA-LITERACY.CCRA.W.8
AASL.I.A.2 AASL.I.B.3 AASL.II.A.2 AASL.IV.B.4 AASL.V.B.1 AASL.
    VI.C.2

You are not alone! There is a way out!

—Sonya Sones

Resources for Sexual Abuse

National Sexual Assault Hotline (24 hours/day)
800-656-HOPE (4673)

RAINN (Rape, Abuse, & Incest National Network)
Visit www.rainn.org.
You can also chat anonymously online in English or Spanish 24/7 at www.rainn
.org/get-help.

Love Is Respect
www.loveisrespect.org
Empowering teens to prevent and end abusive relationships. 24/7 online chat
Confidential phone and text help also available by calling 866-331-9474 or text
loveis to 22522.
There is also a special section on the website geared toward members of the
LGBTQ+ community: www.loveisrepsect.org/is-this-abuse/abusive-lgbtq
-relationships/.

Break the Cycle
www.breakthecycle.org
Inspires and supports those ages 12–24 to build healthy relationships.

***Saving Red* by Sonya Sones**
HarperTeen
October 18, 2016
ISBN: 978-0062370280

Grades: 9 and up

Content Tags:
homelessness, Jewish, mental illness, runaways, suicidal ideation,
therapy dog

Summary

As part of her community service requirement for school, Molly Rosenberg
volunteers to participate in the annual homeless count in Santa Monica. When
she meets Red, Molly is determined to reunite the spirited homeless girl with
her family in time for Christmas. This is easier said than done, as Red is tight
lipped about her past, while Molly has her own things from the past she won't

discuss either. When she realizes Red is exhibiting signs of being mentally ill, she desperately tries to keep her safe until she can figure out how to get Red back to her family. Homelessness in the United States is on the rise, and this complex issue affects people from of all ages and backgrounds. Read what follows to learn more about homelessness and how you can respond to it with your words—and your actions.

Homelessness Poetry Activity

What. The U.S. government defines a homeless person as someone who "lacks a fixed, regular and adequate nighttime residence." But not all homeless people live primarily on the streets. Some people have "unstable housing" and move frequently from place to place. Others often shift from being homeless to having housing—but never have a permanent home. Some homeless individuals and families rely on shelters due to necessity, but many prefer to avoid them because of policies in place.

Why. Poverty continues to be a main cause of homelessness and more than 16 percent of the U.S. population lives in poverty. But specific issues increase potential homelessness for certain groups of teens, including interactions with the criminal justice system and foster care system, sexual orientation, family conflict and violence, teen pregnancy, and mental illness.

Who. People of color and LGBTQI youth are disproportionately represented in the homeless population. There are also specific youth populations who are at greater risk of becoming homeless during their lifetime. And approximately 63 percent of homeless women identify as survivors of domestic violence.

Take action. To take action and help homeless individuals, volunteer at a homeless shelter or soup kitchen near you or donate food and clothes to your local shelter. You can also use your words to advocate for fair housing and legislation that can have a positive impact on the lives of homeless teens.

(Shared with permission from Wiener and PowerPoetry.org, 2019)

Remember that teens have the right to privacy and may not want to share their poetry, but use it for their own self-awareness and catharsis. This activity is meant to look within or to dig deep to think about ways to advocate for others, not to out anyone or make them uncomfortable in any way.

Because homelessness and mental health can be very personal subjects, free verse is a recommended option for this activity.

Curriculum Connections

CCSS.ELA-LITERACY.CCRA.R.3 CCSS.ELA-LITERACY.CCRA.R.4
CCSS.ELA-LITERACY.CCRA.R.6
CCSS.ELA-LITERACY.CCRA.W.1 CCSS.ELA-LITERACY.
CCRA.W.2 CCSS.ELA-LITERACY.CCRA.W.3
CCSS.ELA-LITERACY.CCRA.W.4 CCSS.ELA-LITERACY.
CCRA.W.7 CCSS.ELA-LITERACY.CCRA.W.8
CCSS.ELA-LITERACY.CCRA.W.9 AASL.I.A.2 AASL.I.B.3 AASL.
II.B.2 AASL.II.B.3
AASL.IIIC.2 AASL.IV.A.1 AASL.IV.A.2 AASL.IV.A.3 AASL.IV.C.4
AASL.V.A.2
AASL.VI.2

Resources for the Homeless or Those Suffering from Mental Illness

Homeless Shelter Directory
www.homelessshelterdirectory.org
If you are looking for a safe place to sleep, this directory can help you find the
nearest shelter.

Feeding America
Visit www.feedingamerica.org or call 800-771-2303
If you are hungry, you can type your ZIP code into this website to find a local
food bank.

Free Clinics
www.freeclinics.com
If you are sick, this website will help you find free medical care, wherever you
are.

National Suicide Prevention Lifeline
www.suicidepreventionlifeline.org
If you are in crisis, please call this number right now, 24 hours a day, for help:
800-273-8255.

National Runaway Safeline
www.1800runaway.org or call 800-786-2929
You can share your story 24/7 and get help from someone trained to give the
support you need. All calls are completely confidential.

Miracle Messages
www.miraclemessages.org
This group helps homeless people record short video messages to help them
reunite with their loved ones via social media.

NAMI (National Alliance on Mental Illness)
The largest grassroots mental health organization in the United States, it is dedicated to helping people affected by mental illness, and to obliterating the stigma associated with these diseases.
Call 800-950-6264 or visit https://www.nami.org

Strength of Us
www.strengthofus.org
An online community designed to inspire young adults affected by mental health issues to think positive, stay strong, and achieve their goals through peer support and resource sharing.

A Time to Dance by Padma Venkatraman
Nancy Paulsen Books
May 1, 2014
ISBN: 978-0399257100

Grades: 6 and up

Content Tags:
accidents, amputees, Bharantanatyam, dance, death, disability, Hindu, India, intergenerational, resilience

Summary

Veda, an aspiring Indian teen dancer, thinks she will never dance again after a terrible accident leaves her an amputee from the knee down. Her grandmother, Paati, encourages her to be independent, and she extends her pants and skirts for her while she is on crutches waiting for a prosthetic. Working with her physical therapist, Jim, Veda sees posters of dancers with prosthetics. When Jim tells her, "One day, kiddo, I'll add your poster to my collection," she pursues Bharatanatyam dance with a newfound resilience.

The author's note describes this story as a work of fiction inspired by the life of Smt. Shoba Sharma, who became a performer and dance teacher despite a serious physical injury, along with other dancers who overcame physical trauma, including Smt. Sonal Mansingh, Smt. Sudha Chandran, Sri. Nityananda,

Scan the QR code here for a video featuring Haslet-Davis (*SELF*, 2016), https://www.youtube.com/watch?v=Pf6iaSroltY

and Clayton Bates, who is the disabled Black tap dancer whose photograph Veda sees on Jim's wall. The author also acknowledges Adrianne Haslet-Davis in her dedication, a dancer who became a below-knee amputee like Veda. Haslet-Davis's injury was caused by the Boston Marathon bombing in 2013.

Hopeful Haiku Poetry Activity

When Veda loses her leg in her accident, her hope is restored by the inspiration from the words and actions of those who care about her. Metaphors for hope are often appropriate, as hope itself can be difficult to describe. Hope can lead to resilience . . . having the grit and determination to bounce back despite setbacks. Haslet-Davis, who has a similar journey as Veda, exemplifies this idea.

If you have a good ear for music, you've got a head start in writing haiku. But even if you're not a music fan, don't worry; it's easy to pick up the rhythm of this ancient form of Japanese poetry.

Haiku are short poems that don't rhyme, but instead focus on the total number of syllables in each line. Traditional haiku use a total of 17 syllables spread over three lines of text. Most haiku use a formula of 5-7-5: The first and third lines contain 5 syllables and the middle line contains 7. (Some modern haiku use variations on this formula.)

Haiku-Writing Tips

Choose a topic. Nature is the traditional source of inspiration for haiku, but no topics are off limits. What is something that you know or care a lot about? For example, you can write about your pet, your garage band, or your favorite piece of clothing. Get creative!

Consider the message you'd like to deliver. Why write the poem? What's especially interesting about your topic? Try to think of a twist or an unexpected connection for your reader to consider. For instance, you could write about how your basketball team suffered a terrible losing streak of twenty-five games in a row, but then turned things around, made the playoffs, and won the championship.

Follow the formula. Put some words on the page and count the syllables on each line. Change them around until they match the 5-7-5 syllable structure. Reading your words aloud may help you find the right rhythm.

Use a thesaurus. This tool helps you find synonyms (words that have the same definitions as other words) that will allow you to reach your 5-7-5 syllable count. For instance, the word "nice" has one syllable, "friendly" has two syllables, "sociable" has three syllables, and "personable" has four syllables, but all those words can be used interchangeably.

Center it. Once your haiku is complete, center the text on the page (as opposed to aligning it on the left, as you would for an English paper). That's the traditional way of presenting a haiku.

(Shared with permission from Wiener and PowerPoetry.org, 2019)

Curriculum Connections

CCSS.ELA-LITERACY.CCRA.R.2 CCSS.ELA-LITERACY.CCRA.R.4
CCSS.ELA-LITERACY.CCRA.R.6
CCSS.ELA-LITERACY.CCRA.R.7 CCSS.ELA-LITERACY.CCRA.W.1
CCSS.ELA-LITERACY.CCRA.W.2
CCSS.ELA-LITERACY.CCRA.W.4 AASL.I.A.2 AASL.I.B.3 AASL.
II.A.2 AASL.IV.B.4 AASL.V.B.1
AASL.VI.C.2

Other Words for Home by Jasmine Warga
Balzer + Bray
May 29, 2019
ISBN: 978-0062747808

Grades: 4–8

Content Tags:
Arab American, family dynamics, friendships, immigrants, Islamophobia, Muslim, performing arts, prejudice, racism, refugees, Syria, torn between cultures/places, war

Summary

When things become volatile in war-torn Syria, Jude and her mother take refuge in Cincinnati, Ohio, with relatives, while her father and brother stay behind. Jude finds she has a new label of "Middle Eastern" in the United States, and she struggles to adjust at first. As she begins to make new friends and get to know her new family better, she realizes that she can be herself after all.

Empathy-Building Poetry Activity

Amineh Abou Kerech, a Syrian refugee, has gone through some experiences similar to the protagonist, Jude, in *Other Words for Home*. After fleeing first to Egypt from Syria, Amineh and her family eventually found refuge in England.

This, of course, meant navigating a new culture and also learning a new language, much as Jude did. Amineh used poetry to express herself. Her writing earned her the 2017 Betjeman Poetry Prize in the 10- to 13-year-old category. The thirteen-year-old wrote her prize-winning poem, "Lament for Syria," half in English and half in Arabic. She later translated the full poem into English with help from her

Scan the QR code here for a video of Amineh reciting her prize-winning poetry (Moving Target Films 2017), https://vimeo.com/237486658

teacher, her sister, and Google Translate. Amineh states that she takes words from everywhere, "I take them from songs and films, from what I see on the computer or the television. And I put them all together" (Fox 2017).

Tell students that they will be writing a poem in another language (of the group leader's choice). They are to use free verse and write a five-line poem. Go.

After a minute of confused faces and protests of "I don't know that language," remind them that this is how Jude and Amineh felt trying to write in another language. Discuss empathy and how some of Jude's classmates and even her cousin made her feel bad while she was trying to learn English. Now try that assignment again, this time with help from Google Translate to write it in both English and the alternate language designated. Afterward, ask for volunteers to share theirs aloud, first in English, then the translated version. They are not expected to have correct pronunciation in the alternate language. This is more empathy building, as they experience writing and talking in another language. Encourage more discussion, promoting empathy toward other teens they might know or meet who are going through this type of experience, and brainstorm ways to help those learning new tasks in life.

Curriculum Connections

CCSS.ELA-LITERACY.CCRA.R.3 CCSS.ELA-LITERACY.CCRA.R.4
     CCSS.ELA-LITERACY.CCRA.R.6
CCSS.ELA-LITERACY.CCRA.W.1 CCSS.ELA-LITERACY.
     CCRA.W.2 CCSS.ELA-LITERACY.CCRA.W.3
CCSS.ELA-LITERACY.CCRA.W.4 CCSS.ELA-LITERACY.
     CCRA.W.7 CCSS.ELA-LITERACY.CCRA.W.8
CCSS.ELA-LITERACY.CCRA.W.9 AASL.I.A.2 AASL.I.B.3
     AASL.I.D.3 AASL.II.A.2. AASL.II.A.3
AASL.III.C.3 AASL.IV.A.1 AASL.IV.A.2 AASL.IV.A.3 AASL.B.3
     AASL.V.A.2 AASL.V.B.1

For more information about the Syrian conflict, and to find out how to help refugees like Jude, Warga suggests visiting the following websites:

> https://www.unicefusa.org/mission/emergencies/child-refugees/syria-crisis
> https://www.whitehelmets.org/en
> https://www.doctorswithoutborders.org/what-we-do/countries/syria
> https://my.care.org/site/SPagenavigator/CARE_SpecialDelivery.html
> https://www.refugees-welcome.net
> https://www.icrc.org/en/where-we-work/middle-east/syria

Becoming Billie Holiday by Carole Boston Weatherford
Art by Floyd Cooper
Wordsong
October 1, 2008
ISBN: 978-1590785072

Grades: 8 and up

Content Tags:
addiction, Apollo Theater, Black, body image, Catholicism, death, Great Depression, Harlem, jazz, prostitution, racism, sexual assault/abuse, speakeasies, truancy

Summary

Eleanora Fagan's journey included struggles such as poverty and run-ins with the law. The whole time, Eleanora knew that she had something special: her voice. This fictionalized memoir in verse recounts her metamorphosis into the legendary Billie Holiday.

Moonlight Poetry Activity

Billie Holiday's life was comprised of many challenges, but she kept on singing. Her music is soulful and full of emotions.

Visit the Smithsonian Institution at https://www.si.edu to find these paintings:

Harlem Street Scene with Full Moon by William Johnson (ca. 1939–1940)

Moon over Harlem by William H. Johnson (ca. 1943–1944)

Street Life, Harlem by William H. Johnson (ca. 1939–1940)

Mood is the feeling created by a poet or artist for the reader or observer. While each of these features a moon in a painting set in Harlem, notice that each painting coveys a completely different type of mood. First, play the video/song of Holiday singing "What a Little Moonlight Can Do" (1958). After teens have heard that, have them fold a blank sheet of paper into thirds and label each section 1–3. Post images of the painting on a large screen (or a small screen for a smaller group), one at a time. Pause for a few minutes for each painting, encouraging teens to look at the details of each work of art and write down several words or phrases that describe the mood they sense from the image.

Scan this QR code for a brief video containing rare footage of Billie singing live (Holiday, 1958), https://www.youtube.com/watch?v=R7VNrRS3Sv0.

Next, teens choose which of the three paintings to write about. *Ekphrasis* is a Greek term meaning "description." Therefore, an ekphrastic poem is an expressive description of a scene, or more typically, a work of art. The poet can expand its meaning with vivid, eloquent reflections of the piece.

Use the following tips to guide writing an ekphrastic poem:

- Look at the artwork, from different angles. Be mindful of how it makes you feel. Take notes about your thoughts and use multiple senses to help describe them.

- Who do you see in the painting? What are they doing? What might their conversation be about?

Because this an ekphrastic activity focusing on the mood of the art, any poetic form can be used. Free verse, haiku, sonnet, cinquain, concrete, contrapuntal—whichever one that the poet feels expresses the mood best. After teens have finished writing, choose volunteers to read their poems aloud and have the rest of the group guess which painting their poem was about. If time permits, teens can choose a different painting and do the activity again to compare and contrast their two poems.

Curriculum Connections

CCSS.ELA-LITERACY.CCRA.R.3 CCSS.ELA-LITERACY.CCRA.R.4
CCSS.ELA-LITERACY.CCRA.R.6
CCSS.ELA-LITERACY.CCRA.W.1 CCSS.ELA-LITERACY.
CCRA.W.2 CCSS.ELA-LITERACY.CCRA.W.3

CCSS.ELA-LITERACY.CCRA.W.4 CCSS.ELA-LITERACY.
CCRA.W.7 CCSS.ELA-LITERACY.CCRA.W.8
CCSS.ELA-LITERACY.CCRA.W.9 AASL.I.A.2 AASL.I.B.3 AASL.
II.A.2 AASL.IV.B.4
AASL.V.B.1 AASL.VI.C.2

White Rose by Kip Wilson
Versify
April 2, 2019
ISBN: 978-1328594433

Grades: 7 and up

Content Tags:
Blitzkrieg, death, first love/sex, German, Holocaust, Jewish, Kristallnacht, Nazi resistance, rebellion

Summary

Sophie Scholl and her brother write and distribute anonymous letters criticizing the Nazi regime and informing their fellow German citizens of the truth about what was happening. The next year, the two of them were arrested for treason and interrogated to provide information about their collaborators in this rebellion. This novel in verse reports on their lives and their brave stance against the Nazis.

Zine Poetry Activity

Sophie and her brother passed out zines in letter form to protest the Nazi regime. A *zine* (short for *magazine* or *fanzine*) is a self-published booklet that you make yourself of whatever you want, which you then photocopy to either sell or give away. Generally, they are created by a single person or a very small group. Sometimes you may hear poets call them "chapbooks," but the term *zine* is more common today. The purpose of zines is that you can say essentially whatever you want and put it out there without having to go through a go-between for approval or funding. Because of this, zines are often used as protests about a given topic. (For more on protest poetry, find *Soaring Earth* by Engle in the Author/Title Index.)

Choose a topic of concern to create a title and protest poetry about. Formats like diamante, concrete, or others may be especially powerful, as they provide a visual along with your words, but any format each poet feels works with the words is fine for this activity. The aesthetic can also be changed with words or phrases cut out from magazines or by changing the appearance of the text: bold, italics, size variations, color, or other options. Because teens are creating booklets and not just a single poem, this activity can take place over more than one day.

Once the poems are ready, decide on a sequence for them. If your poems form a continuing narrative (such as in novels in verse), this is very important. If each poem is an individual thought via a separate piece of work, there may be more flexibility with sequencing.

Photocopying can be tricky, especially with front/back pages and keeping the correct sequence. Teachers and librarians are great at helping with this, so funds are not lost on unusable copies. Collate and staple the booklets when finished. A long-arm stapler often works best with thicker groupings of papers. If you don't have a long-armed stapler, you can try and do the task with a normal one by folding the paper; but this often doesn't work. If so, use a big rubber band on each zine, sew the booklets together, or use a hole puncher and bind it with either book rings, yarn, or ribbon.

Now, the zine needs a cover. If you have any unique, fancy, or colored paper, this can help it stand out. Another option is to cut up old, leftover rolls of wallpaper for a thicker, more protective cover. Be sure to include the title and author name on the front.

Curriculum Connections

CCSS.ELA-LITERACY.CCRA.R.2 CCSS.ELA-LITERACY.CCRA.R.3 CCSS.ELA-LITERACY.CCRA.R.4

CCSS.ELA-LITERACY.CCRA.R.6 CCSS.ELA-LITERACY.CCRA.R.7 CCSS.ELA-LITERACY.CCRA.W.1

CCSS.ELA-LITERACY.CCRA.W.2 CCSS.ELA-LITERACY. CCRA.W.3 CCSS.ELA-LITERACY.CCRA.W.4

CCSS.ELA-LITERACY.CCRA.W.7 CCSS.ELA-LITERACY. CCRA.W.8 CCSS.ELA-LITERACY.CCRA.W.9

AASL.I.A.2 AASL.I.B.3 AASL.I.D.1 AASL.I.D.3 AASL.II.B.2 AASL. II.C.2 AASL.III.C.2

AASL.III.D.2 AASL.IV.D.2 AASL.V.A.2 AASL.V.B.1 AASL.V.C.1 AASL.VI.C.2

Brown Girl Dreaming by Jacqueline Woodson
Nancy Paulsen Books
August 28, 2014
ISBN: 978-0399252518

Grades: 5 and up

Content Tags:
Black, Civil Rights Era/Movement, death, double Dutch, ice cream truck, intergenerational, Jehovah's Witnesses, Jim Crow, music, racism, religion, torn between cultures/places, writing

Summary

Jacqueline Woodson's memoir in verse has family at its heart. Summers in the South with her grandparents bring crickets, frogs, and owls singing a lullaby, while time with her mother in Brooklyn involves double Dutch, music without the word *funk* in it, and the Kingdom Hall. She genuinely loves both places and wishes for a way to have one *and* the other. As she begins her journey becoming a writer, she realizes that "YOU decide what each world and each story and each ending will finally be."

Ode to Family Poetry Activity

All my life, my family has been giving me the gifts of books and story and experiences that helped me write not only Brown Girl Dreaming, but everything I've ever written. So the book feels like an ode to family—to the people who showed me how the ordinary is quite extraordinary and that our history is what buoys us and keeps us moving forward.

(Woodson, quoted in Parrott and Toth, 2015)

When Woodson was asked why she wrote *Brown Girl Dreaming* in verse format, she replied, "This is how memory comes to me—in small moments with all of this white space around them. I didn't think this memoir could be told any other way. It felt like it would be untrue to the story to try to write a straight narrative our of lyrical memory" (Vardell 2015b).

Given Woodson's comments regarding her family and how the memories came to her in small moments, teens will use that style to create an "Ode to Family" poem. An ode is a poem that is about one specific thing that you think is really amazing and worthy of praise. This type of poem can be focused on a person, an object, or even something abstract like an idea or a feeling. First, teens take out a sheet of paper and create three columns. Label them "Past," "Present," and "Future." Each teen then created their own list of memories that come to them from each time period (the future being what they think will come next or goals of what they want to come next).

Follow these steps to create your "Ode to Family":

- Pick some memories from your list that you feel strongly about, so you have enough to write. If you feel something, write something. When someone brings up the thing you have chosen to write about in conversation, how do you react? Write down what you would say in such a situation, and even more importantly, how you would (or do) feel. You may end up needing many words that have the same definition or meaning, so checking out a thesaurus can be hugely useful. Learning how to write an ode poem is all about digging deep into your emotional and descriptive vocabulary.

- How long do you want your poem to be? Odes are traditionally very long, and chances are, if you've picked a topic you really feel passionately about, you will have a lot to write. Start by splitting up your poem into groups, or stanzas, of ten lines. Many traditional odes have three to five of these stanzas, but if you want to write more, by all means do!

- To rhyme or not to rhyme? Do you want your poem to rhyme? Most odes do, and making your ode rhyme would be a fun challenge, but you can also write irregular odes, which don't have to rhyme or maintain a perfect rhythm. If you do decide to make your ode rhyme, think about how you want to format the rhyme scheme of this poem. You can make every two lines or every other line rhyme. You can also make up your own pattern—just commit to it, and use it in every stanza of your ode poem.

(Shared with permission from Wiener and PowerPoetry.org, 2019)

If your ode is written about a particular person, you could give it to them as a gift. You can recite your ode, or you can put it to music and sing it. Privacy is respected, as always, when it comes to personal information in poetry.

Curriculum Connections

CCSS.ELA-LITERACY.CCRA.R.2 CCSS.ELA-LITERACY.CCRA.R.4
CCSS.ELA-LITERACY.CCRA.R.6
CCSS.ELA-LITERACY.CCRA.R.7 CCSS.ELA-LITERACY.CCRA.W.1
CCSS.ELA-LITERACY.CCRA.W.2
CCSS.ELA-LITERACY.CCRA.W.4 AASL.I.A.2 AASL.B.3 AASL.
II.B.3 AASL.III.C.2 AASL.IV.B.4
AASL.V.B.1 AASL.VI.C.2

Finding Baba Yaga by Jane Yolen
Tor
October 30, 2018
ISBN: 978-1250163875

Grades: 8 and up

Content Tags:
American realism, cousins, family dynamics, folklore, humor, runaways,
Russian

Summary

You may *think* you know the story of Baba Yaga . . . but you don't. When Natasha gathers her strength to leave her harsh, controlling father, she comes upon the magical house in the woods . . . the legendary one that walks on chicken feet with a fairy-tale witch inside. The theme of a young woman discovering the power to take control of her fate and speak up is both timely and timeless.

Imagery Prompt Poetry Activity

Imagery abounds in *Finding Baba Yaga*. Imagery is the process of using vivid, descriptive words to give the reader a detailed picture of what is going on in your writing so that they can easily picture, or visualize, it in their own mind. The chapter called "I See the Bony Hand First" introduces what happens after a knock, knock at the door:

> I see the bony hand first,
> knuckles broken on the wall of time.
> Dirt under long fingernails,
> It signals me in.

Use the first line as a writing prompt to create creepy poems using imagery and personification. The poetic form is decided by the group leader. Ask volunteers to share their work aloud when finished.

Curriculum Connections

CCSS.ELA-LITERACY.CCRA.R.1 CCSS.ELA-LITERACY.CCRA.R.4
    CCSS.ELA-LITERACY.CCRA.R.6
CCSS.ELA-LITERACY.CCRA.W.3 CCSS.ELA-LITERACY.
    CCRA.W.4 AASL.I.A.1 AASL.I.A.2
AASL.I.B.3 AASL.II.B.3 AASL.III.A.1 AASL.IV.B.2 AASL.IV.B.4
    AASL.V.B.1 AASL.VI.C.2

Glossary of Poetic Devices

Words are weapons. Your words can change the way people that look at the world and even inspire action. Browse some ideas for ways that you can use a poem to make a difference. (Glossary shared with permission from Weiner and PowerPoetry.org, 2019)

Alliteration
Alliteration is the repetition of the same first letter or sound in a group of words.

Allusion
An allusion is an indirect reference to something.

Anthropomorphism
Anthropomorphism is when anything nonhuman, such as an animal or object, is given human qualities, including emotions and actions.

Assonance
Assonance occurs in a sentence when two or more words near each other have the same vowel sounds but start with different consonants.

Chiasmus
Chiasmus is a figure of speech that has two phrases that are parallel and opposite.

Connotation
Connotation is an association that you make automatically with a word, including how the word makes you feel.

Deus ex machina
Deus ex machina is when an unlikely character, object, ability, or idea is introduced into a story in order to end the main conflict and solve any lingering problems quickly.

Epistrophe
Epistrophe is the repetition of a word or phrase at the end of successive clauses, sentences, or verses.

Euphemism
Euphemism is when harsh words or phrases with more mild ones to soften the blow of something that could have a more negative connotation otherwise.

Hyperbole
Hyperbole is when certain words are used in a phrase to exaggerate an idea.

Imagery
Imagery is the process of using vivid, descriptive words to give readers a detailed picture of what is going on in writing so that they can easily picture, or visualize, it in their own minds.

Juxtaposition
Juxtaposition is when two (sometimes completely opposite) words are placed near one another, creating a comparison/contrast effect.

Litote
A litote is a nice, almost secretive understatement saying something negative or unpleasant without any negative/unpleasant words used in the statement.

Malapropism
Malapropism occurs when a word that fits the context of a sentence is substituted with another, incorrect word.

Metaphor
A metaphor is when a word or phrase for one thing is used in place of another in order to make a comparison between two unlike things and indirectly suggest a similarity.

Metonymy
Metonymy occurs when a word or phrase is replaced with a different one with which it is associated.

Onomatopoeia
Onomatopoeia occurs when the sound that a word makes mimics what the word means.

Oxymoron
Oxymoron occurs when two contradictory words are placed next to one another.

Repetition
Repetition is when a word or sentence is used more than once within a poem.

Rhyme scheme
Rhyme scheme refers to the particular lines in a piece of poetry that rhyme, usually by using words at the end of each line that sound similar.

Simile
A simile is a figure of speech using "like" or "as" to compare one thing to another thing of a different kind.

Synecdoche
Synecdoche is when a part of something represents the whole, or vice versa.

Synonym
A synonym is a word with the same or close to the same meaning as another word.

Verisimilitude
Verisimilitude refers to when a piece of work appears true and realistic.

Works Cited

Acevedo, Elizabeth. *The Poet X*. New York: PUSH, 2018.

Adichie, Chimamanda N. 2009. "The Danger of a Single Story." Filmed in July at TEDGlobal. Video, 18:35. https://www.ted.com/talks/chimamanda_adichie_the_danger_of_a_single_story.

Alexander, Kwame. *The Crossover*. New York: HMH Books for Young Readers, 2014.

Alexander, Kwame. *Booked*. New York: HMH Books for Young Readers, 2016.

Alexander, Kwame. *Solo*. New York: HMH Books for Young Readers, 2017.

Alexander, Kwame. *Rebound*. New York: HMH Books for Young Readers, 2018.

American University. National Antiracist Book Festival. Accessed August 21, 2019. https://www.american.edu/centers/antiracism/book-fair.

Anderson, Laurie H. *Shout*. New York: Viking Books for Young Readers, 2019.

Association for Library Services to Children. About the Children's Literature Legacy Award. Accessed September 14, 2018. http://www.ala.org/alsc/awardsgrants/bookmedia/clla/about.

Barker, Wendy, K. Clark, R. Dove, J. Galassi, and K. Young. 2013. "Staggered Tellings: Immediacy, Intimacy, and Ellipses in the Verse Novel." Panel presentation at the Association of Writers and Writing Programs Conference, Boston, March 7.

Bennett, Tamryn. "Comics Poetry: Beyond 'Sequential Art'." *Image & Narrative* 15, no. 2 (2014): 106–123. http://www.imageandnarrative.be/index.php/imagenarrative/article/download/544/397.

Bishop, Rudine Sims. "Mirrors, Windows, and Sliding Glass Doors." *Perspectives* 6, no. 3 (Summer 1990): ix–xi.

Blay, Amanda, and C. Brown. 2019. "Engaging Student Interests by Using New and Diverse Texts." *Engage Now* (blog), National Council of Teachers of English, January 11. https://www2.ncte.org/blog/2019/01/engaging-student-interests-by-using-new-and-diverse-texts.

Bloome, David. 2018. Keynote speech at the Virginia Hamilton Multicultural Literature Conference, Kent, OH, October 13.

BPLvideos. 2011. "Brooklyn Public Library: Why I Love My Library." YouTube video, May 10, 1:50. https://www.youtube.com/watch?v=SCagg1FRU68.

Bowles, David. *They Call Me Güero: A Border Kid's Poems.* El Paso, TX: Cinco Puntos Press, 2018.

Brewer, Robert L. 2017. "Contrapuntal Poem: Poetic Form." *Writer's Digest*, February 6. https://www.writersdigest.com/writing-articles/contrapuntal -poem-poetic-form.

Bridges, Stephanie. 2014. "How Poetry Can Help Your Addiction Recovery." *Addiction Blog*, American Addiction Centers, May 8. https://addictionblog.org /mind/how-poetry-can-help-your-addiction-recovery.

Brown, Jeffrey. 2007. "The Poem as Comic Strip #3." *Poetry Foundation*, May 21. https://www.poetryfoundation.org/articles/68881/the-poem-as-comic -strip-3.

Bueher, Jennifer. 2010. "Their Lives Are Beautiful, Too: How Matt Dela Pena Illuminates the Lives of Urban Teens." *Alan Review* 37 (2): 36–43.

Cadden, Mike. "The Verse Novel and the Question of Genre." *The ALAN Review* 39, no. 1 (Fall 2011): 21–27. https://doi.org/10.21061/alan.v39i1.a.3.

Camilo, Michel. 2011. "Michel Camilo—Watermelon Man." Shared by ScrewFbook, YouTube video, March 11, 4:28. https://www.youtube.com/watch?v =HVhFGumwdBI.

Campbell, Patty. "The Sand in the Oyster: Vetting the Verse Novel." *Horn Book Magazine,* 80 (2004): 611–616.

Children's Cooperative Book Center, School of Education. 2019. "Publishing Statistics on Children's/YA Books About People of Color and First/Native Nations and by People of Color and First/Native Nations Authors and Illustrators." Madison: University of Wisconsin-Madison (July 5). http:// ccbc.education.wisc.edu/books/pcstats.asp.

Clark, Kristin E. *Freakboy.* New York: Farrar, Straus and Giroux Books for Younger Readers, 2013.

Corrigan, Eireann. *You Remind Me of You: A Poetry Memoir.* New York: PUSH, 2002.

Digital Video Technology Suncoast Technical College. 2015. "Tuskegee Airmen; A Short Biography." YouTube video, May 18, 3:54. https://www.youtube .com/watch?v=bcFEwgoWymo.

Dimmig, Brenda. *Sanctuary Somewhere.* New York: West 44 Books, 2019.

Dunbar, Paul Laurence. 2006. "We Wear the Mask." *Poets.org*, February 17. https:// poets.org/poem/we-wear-mask.

Dunbar-Ortiz, Roxanne. *An Indigenous People's History of the United States for Young People.* Adapted by Jean Mendoza and Debbie Reese. Boston: Beacon Press, 2019.

Ebarvia, Tricia. 2018a. "Disrupting Texts as a Restorative Practice." *Triciaebarvia .org*, July 11. https://triciaebarvia.org/2018/07/11/disrupting-texts-as-a -restorative-practice.

Ebarvia, Tricia. 2018b. "Strategies to Dig Deeper: Writing Into and Out of Discomfort with Our Students and Ourselves Through Identity and Perspective-Taking." *Triciaebarvia.org*, June 29. https://triciaebarvia.org /2018/06/29/strategies-to-dig-deeper.

Ebarvia, Tricia. "Disrupting Your Texts: Why Simply Including Diverse Voices Is Not Enough." *Literacy Today* 37, no. 1 (July/August 2019): 40–41. https://triciaebarvia.org/2019/07/18/why-diverse-texts-are-not-enough.

Engle, Margarita. *The Lightning Dreamer: Cuba's Greatest Abolitionist.* New York: Harcourt, 2013.

Engle, Margarita. *Enchanted Air: Two Cultures, Two Wings: A Memoir.* New York: Atheneum Books for Young Readers, 2015.

Engle, Margarita. *Jazz Owls: A Novel of the Zoot Suit Riots.* New York: Atheneum Books for Young Readers, 2018.

Engle, Margarita. *Soaring Earth.* New York: Atheneum Books for Young Readers, 2019.

Engle, Margarita. *With a Star in My Hand: Ruben Dario, Poetry Hero.* New York: Atheneum Books for Young Readers, 2019.

Farish, Terry. *The Good Braider.* New York: Skyscape, 2012.

Farish, Terry. "Why Verse? Poetic Novels for Historical Fiction, Displacement Stories, and Struggling Readers." *School Library Journal* 59, no. 11 (2013): 32–33.

First Book. 2019. "Now Streaming the Discussion ON YOUTH with Authors Jason Reynolds and Jacqueline Woodson LIVE from the National Antiracist Book Festival at American University in Washington, DC." Facebook, April 27. https://www.facebook.com/FirstBook/videos/336735357198385.

Flake, Sharon G. "Who Says Black Boys Won't Read?" *Journal of Children's Literature* 34, no. 1 (2007): 13–14.

Fox, Killian. "The 13-Year-Old Syrian Refugee Who Became a Prizewinning Poet." *Observer Magazine, The Guardian*, October 1, 2017. https://www.theguardian.com/books/2017/oct/01/the-13-year-old-syrian-refugee-prizewinning-poet-amineh-abou-kerech-betjeman-prize.

Frank, Lucy. *Two Girls Staring at the Ceiling.* New York: Schwartz and Wade, 2014.

Freyn, Amy L. "Effects of a Multimodal Approach on ESL/EFL University Students' Attitudes Towards Poetry." *Journal of Education and Practice* 8, no. 8 (2017): 80–83. https://files.eric.ed.gov/fulltext/EJ1139053.pdf.

Gellman, Lucy. 2017. "Spoken Word for Trans Rights." YouTube video, March 28, 3:26. https://www.youtube.com/watch?v=1bcgXyc5nm8.

Goucher College. n.d. *The "Canon" of English Literature.* Accessed August 21, 2019. http://faculty.goucher.edu/eng211/canon_of_english_literature.htm.

Grimes, Nikki. *Bronx Masquerade.* New York: Dial Books, 2002.

Grimes, Nikki. *Between the Lines.* New York: Nancy Paulsen Books, 2018.

Grimes, Nikki. *Garvey's Choice.* Westminster, MD: Wordsong, 2019.

Grimes, Nikki. *Ordinary Hazards.* Westminister, MD: Wordsong, 2019.

Hancock, Herbie. 2010. "Watermelon Man." Shared by Jazzman2696, YouTube video, March 21, 6:31. https://www.youtube.com/watch?v=4bjPlBC4h_8.

Harrison, Cynthia. 2012. "Braided Poems." October 25. https://cynthiaharrison.com/2012/10/25/braided-poems.

Holiday, Billie. 2010. "Billie Holiday—What a Little Moonlight Can Do—1958 LIVE.avi." Shared by KING4DANIELLA, YouTube video, June 23, 3:08. https://www.youtube.com/watch?v=R7VNrRS3Sv0.

Holt, K. A. *House Arrest*. San Francisco: Chronicle, 2015.

Holt, K. A. *Knock Out*. San Francisco: Chronicle, 2018.

Holt, K. A. *Redwood and Ponytail*. San Francisco: Chronicle, 2019.

Hopkins, Ellen. *Crank*. New York: Margaret K. McElderry Books, 2004.

Hopkins, Ellen. *Glass*. New York: Margaret K. McElderry Books, 2007.

Hopkins, Ellen. *Fallout*. New York: Margaret K. McElderry Books, 2010.

Horrocks, Dana. 2013. "Talking Genres: Verse Novels." YouTube video, March 25, 2:10. https://youtu.be/LXViVD7LQAM.

Hughes, Langston. "Dreams." In *The Collected Poems of Langston Hughes*. New York: Alfred A. Knopf/Vintage, 1994. Available at https://poets.org/poem/dreams.

Hughes, Langston. "Harlem." In *The Collected Works of Langston Hughes*. Columbia: University of Missouri Press, 2002. Available at https://www.poetryfoundation.org/poems/46548/harlem.

Hughes-Hassell, Sandra. "Mirror and Window Books: *Why* and *How*." Independent School Round Table, Charlotte Country Day School, Charlotte, NC, March 2017. http://libequity.web.unc.edu/presentations-about-equity-issues/mirror-and-window-books-why-and-how.

Hughes-Hassell, Sandra. "Multicultural Young Adult Literature as a Form of Counter-Storytelling." *The Library Quarterly: Information, Community, Policy* 83, no. 3 (July 2013): 212–228. https://doi.org/10.1086/670696.

Huyck, David, and Sarah Park Dahlen. 2019. "Diversity in Children's Books 2018." *sarahpark.com* (blog), June 19. Created in consultation with Edith Campbell, Molly Beth Griffin, K. T. Horning, Debbie Reese, Ebony Elizabeth Thomas, and Madeline Tyner, with statistics compiled by the Cooperative Children's Book Center, School of Education, University of Wisconsin-Madison: http://ccbc.education.wisc.edu/books/pcstats.asp. Retrieved from https://readingspark.wordpress.com/2019/06/19/picture-this-diversity-in-childrens-books-2018-infographic.

I Am From Project. 2018. "Welcome." January 17, https://iamfromproject.com.

James, Rory. *Some Girls Bind*. Berkeley Heights, NJ: Enslow, 2019.

Jensen, Karen. 2017. "Diversity Considerations in YA: Doing a Diversity Audit." *Teen Librarian Toolbox* (blog), *School Library Journal*. http://www.teenlibrariantoolbox.com/files/2017/11/Diversity-Audit-Outline-2017-with-Sources.pdf.

Jensen, Karen. 2019a. "A Brief History of YA Literature, an Infographic." *Teen Librarian Toolbox* (blog). *School Library Journal*, July 25. http://www.teenlibrariantoolbox.com/2019/07/a-brief-history-of-ya-literature-an-infographic.

Jensen, Karen. 2019b. "Equity in Action: Building Inclusive Collections and Services." SLJTeen*Live!* Virtual Summit, August 8.

Jewett, Michelle. "Speaking Truth to Power: Whitesplaining the Canon." *English Journal* 106, no. 5 (May 2017): 95–98.

Judge, Lita. *Mary's Monster: Love, Madness, and How Mary Shelley Created Frankenstein*. New York: Roaring Brook Press, 2018.

Kentucky Arts Council. 2018. "Kentucky's "Where I'm From": A Poetry of Place."
  Kentucky.gov, November 9. http://artscouncil.ky.gov/KAC/Vibrant/Where
  FromAbout.htm.

King, Albert. 2012. "Albert King—Watermelon Man." Shared by djclay33, YouTube
  video, June 10, 4:03. https://www.youtube.com/watch?v=6u669AlN5E8.

Krok, Lisa. 2019. "Fight the Power: Music as a Social Force, a Guest Post by Lisa
  Krok." *Teen Librarian Toolbox* (blog), *School Library Journal*, February 13.
  http://www.teenlibrariantoolbox.com/2019/02/fight-the-power-music-as
  -a-social-force-a-guest-post-by-lisa-krok.

Kuderick, Madeleine. *Kiss of Broken Glass*. New York: HarperTeen, 2014.

Kumasi, Kafi, and Sandra Hughes-Hassell. "Shifting Lenses on Youth Literacy &
  Identity." *Knowledge Quest* 45, no. 3 (January/February 2017): 12–21.
  https://files.eric.ed.gov/fulltext/EJ1125480.pdf.

Lai, Thanhha. *Inside Out and Back Again*. New York: HarperCollins, 2011.

Lee and Low Books. 2017. "Classroom Library Questionnaire." *Educator Resources*,
  https://www.leeandlow.com/uploads/loaded_document/408/Classroom
  -Library-Questionnaire_FINAL.pdf.

Lee, Cassy. "Fostering Empathy Through Library Programming and Collaboration." SLJTeen*Live!* Virtual Summit, August 8, 2019.

Letcher, Mark. "Off the Shelves: Poetry and Verse Novels for Young Adults." *The
  English Journal* 99, no. 3 (2010), 87–90. https://www.jstor.org/stable/4050
  3490.

Lindberg, Maya. "Tell Transgender Students: We're Still Here for You." *Teaching Tolerance Magazine*, February 23, 2017. https://www.tolerance.org/magazine
  /tell-transgender-students-were-still-here-for-you.

Lowitz, Leza. *Up from the Sea*. New York: Crown Books for Young Readers,
  2016.

Lyon, George Ella. 1993. "Where I'm From." Read by the author. http://www
  .georgeellalyon.com/audio/where.mp3.

Lyon, George Ella. 2015. "Where I'm From." March 27. http://www.georgeellalyon
  .com/where.html.

McCall, Guadalupe G. *Under the Mesquite*. New York: Lee and Low Books,
  2011.

McCullough, Joy. *Blood Water Paint*. New York: Dutton Books for Young Readers,
  2018.

McGhee, Alison. *What I Leave Behind*. New York: Atheneum/Caitlyn Dlouhy Books,
  2018.

Meany. 2009. "Meany—Swan Lake." Shared by hallsterr, YouTube video, February 5, 3:55. https://www.youtube.com/watch?v=d6UfySXJ6K0.

Metropolitan Museum of Art. 2019. Home page. https://www.metmuseum.org.

Moving Target Films. 2017. "Amineh—Lament for Syriah with Text." Vimeo video,
  2:17. https://vimeo.com/237486658.

Myers, Walter D. *Street Love*. New York: Amistad Press, 2007.

Myers, Walter D. *Amiri & Odette: A Love Story*. New York: Scholastic, 2009.

Myers, Walter D. "Where Are the People of Color in Children's Books?" *The New York Times*, March 15, 2014. https://www.nytimes.com/2014/03/16/opinion/sunday/where-are-the-people-of-color-in-childrens-books.html.

Nelson, Marilyn. *How I Discovered Poetry*. New York: Dial Books, 2014.

Nelson, Marilyn. *American Ace*. New York: Dial Books, 2016.

Nesbitt, Kenn. 2011. "How to Write a Diamante Poem." *Poetry4Kids.com*, November 17. https://www.poetry4kids.com/lessons/how-to-write-a-diamante-poem.

Nesbitt, Kenn. 2016. "How to Start a Poetry Journal." *Poetry4Kids.com*, September 26. https://www.poetry4kids.com/lessons/how-to-start-a-poetry-journal.

Parker, Kim. "High School Matters: Beyond Single Literacy Stories." *English Journal, High School Edition* 103, no. 4 (March 2014): 16–17.

Parrott, Kiera, and Luann Toth. "Jacqueline Woodson on Weaving Memory, Crafting Poetry, and Writing for Young Adults." *School Library Journal*, January 2015. https://www.slj.com/?detailStory=jacqueline-woodson-on-weaving-memory-crafting-poetry-and-writing-for-young-adults.

Penguin Random House Audio. 2019. "Laurie Halse Anderson on Narrating SHOUT." YouTube video, April 15, 2019, 0:41. https://www.youtube.com/watch?v=ttzJR5tGTTA.

Poetry Foundation. 2019. "Collection: Poems of Protest, Resistance, and Empowerment." *PoetryFoundation.org*. https://www.poetryfoundation.org/collections/101581/poems-of-protest-resistance-and-empowerment.

Poetry Slam Inc. 2016. "Women of the World Poetry Slam 2016—Elizabeth Acevedo 'Hair'." YouTube, May 21, 2:20. https://youtu.be/J-DrDINervE.

Poets.org. 2004. "Play Exquisite Corpse." https://poets.org/text/play-exquisite-corpse.

Powell, Patricia Hruby. *Loving vs. Virginia: A Documentary Novel of the Landmark Civil Rights Case*. San Francisco: Chronicle, 2017.

"Puerto Rican Bomba Dance—Sanse 2017." 2017. Shared by aureliofont, YouTube video, February 18, 1:18. https://www.youtube.com/watch?v=x3Gkta-3Jzw.

Pushpa, V. K., and S. Y. Savaedi. "Teaching Poetry in Autonomous ELT Classes." *Procedia—Social and Behavioral Sciences* 98 (2014): 1919–1925. https://core.ac.uk/download/pdf/82476982.pdf.

Quintero, Isabel. *Gabi, a Girl in Pieces*. El Paso, TX: Cinco Puntos Press, 2014.

Raybuck, Dorie. "Field Notes: 'This Is Too Much!' Why Verse Novels Work for Reluctant Readers." *The Horn Book Magazine* (March/April 2015). https://www.hbook.com/2015/03/featured/field-notes-this-is-too-much-why-verse-novels-work-for-reluctant-readers.

Reynolds, Jason. *Long Way Down*. New York: Atheneum/Caitlyn Dlouhy Books, 2017.

Reynolds, Jason. *For Every One*. New York: Atheneum/Caitlyn Dlouhy Books, 2018.

Salazar, Aida. *The Moon Within*. New York: Arthur A. Levine, 2019.

Salfia, Jessica. 2018. "Write to Fight." *West Virginia Council of Teachers of English* (blog), October 11. https://wvcte.com/2018/10/11/write-to-fight.

Sanchez, Diego. 2018. "Free, Printable Comic Strip Templates." *Comic* (blog), MediaLoot.com, February 7. https://medialoot.com/blog/free-printable -comic-strip-templates.

Santamaria, Mongo. 2013. "Mongo Santamaria—Watermelon Man (1963)." Shared by windmillsofmusic, YouTube video, January 12, 3:15. https://www .youtube.com/watch?v=I43vckpRjMk.

SELF. 2016. "Boston Marathon Survivor Adrianne Haslet on Dancing Through Life | Body Stories | SELF." YouTube video, October 12, 3:27. https://www .youtube.com/watch?v=Pf6iaSroItY.

Shmoop Editorial Team. "We Wear the Mask Form and Meter." Shmoop University, Inc. Last modified November 11, 2008; accessed September 2, 2019. https://www.shmoop.com/we-wear-the-mask/rhyme-form-meter.html.

Simonov, Yuri and London Philharmonic Orchestra. 2012. "Tchaikovsky—Swan Lake (Swan Theme)." Shared by pianushko, YouTube video, May 21, 2:59. https://www.youtube.com/watch?v=9cNQFB0TDfY.

Smithsonian Institution. 2019. Home page. https://www.si.edu.

Sones, Sonya. *Saving Red*. New York: HarperTeen, 2016.

Sones, Sonya. *The Opposite of Innocent*. New York: HarperTeen, 2018.

StVil, Lola. *Girls Like Me*. New York: HMH Books for Young Readers, 2016.

Styslinger, Mary. *Workshopping the Canon*. Urbana, IL: National Council of Teachers of English, 2017.

Tatum, Beverly D. "The ABC Approach to Creating Climates of Engagement on Diverse Campuses." *Liberal Education* 86, no. 4 (2000): 22–29.

Thomas, Ebony Elizabeth. "African American Children's Literature: Liminal Terrains and Strategies for Selfhood." In *Diversity in Youth Literature: Opening Doors Through Reading*, edited by J. Naidoo and S. Park, 33–34. New York: ALA Editions, 2013.

Thomas, Ebony Elizabeth. *The Dark Fantastic: Race and the Imagination from Harry Potter to the Hunger Games*. New York: NYU Press, 2019.

Thomas, Ebony Elizabeth, Debbie Reese, and Teri S. Lesesne. "Right to Read: (Re) envisioning and (Re)reading: Examining Problematic Texts." *The ALAN Review* 42, no. 3 (Summer 2015): 68–72.

Torres, Christina. 2019. "The Power of Words: On 'Classics' and 'Canon'." *The Intersection: Culture and Race in Schools* (blog). *Education Week Teacher*, April 16. https://blogs.edweek.org/teachers/intersection-culture-and-race -in-education/2019/04/the_power_of_words_on_classics_and_canon .html.

Vardell, Sylvia M. 2015a. "Classroom Connections: Diverse Verse." *Book Links* 111 (supplement), *Booklist* (January): 27–31. https://www.booklistonline.com /Classroom-Connections-Diverse-Verse-Sylvia-M-Vardell/pid=7208787.

Vardell, Sylvia M. 2015b. "Classroom Connections: Memoirs in Verse." *Book Links* (supplement), *Booklist* (April): 22–25. https://www.booklistonline.com /Classroom-Connections-Memoirs-in-Verse-Sylvia-M-Vardell/pid=737 8013.

Venkatraman, Padma. *A Time to Dance*. New York: Nancy Paulsen Books, 2014.

Vezzali, L., S. Stathi, and D. Giovannini. "Indirect Contact Through Book Reading: Improving Adolescents' Attitudes and Behavioral Intentions Toward Immigrants." *Psychology in the Schools,* 49 (2012), 148–162. doi:10.1002/pits.20621.

Warga, Jasmine. *Other Words for Home*. New York: Balzer + Bray, 2019.

We Need Diverse Books. 2014. "We Need Diverse Books Campaign Video." YouTube Video, October 27, 4:11. https://youtu.be/mrrh0G-OkBw.

We Need Diverse Books. 2017. "About WNDB." DiverseBooks.org, December 15. https://diversebooks.org/about-wndb.

Weatherford, Carole B. *Becoming Billie Holiday*. Westminster, MD: Wordsong, 2008.

Wiener, Jennifer, and PowerPoetry.org. 2019. "The Largest Mobile/Online Teen Poetry Community." PowerPoetry.org. https://www.powerpoetry.org

Williams, William Carlos. "This Is Just to Say." 1962. https://poets.org/poem/just-say.

Wilson, Kip. *White Rose*. New York: Versify, 2019.

Woodson, Jacqueline. *Brown Girl Dreaming*. New York: Nancy Paulsen Books, 2014.

Yale's Voke Spoken Word Group. 2017. "Spoken Word for Trans Rights." Shared by Lucy Gellman, You Tube video, March 28, 3:26. https://www.youtube.com/watch?v=1bcgXyc5nm8

Yolen, Jane. *Finding Baba Yaga*. New York: Tor Books, 2018.

Young Adult Library Services Association. "Quick Picks for Reluctant Young Adult Readers." http://www.ala.org/yalsa/quick-picks-reluctant-young-adult-readers.

Young Adult Library Services Association. "Quick Picks for Reluctant Young Adult Readers: Selection Criteria." http://www.ala.org/yalsa/booklistsawards/booklists/quickpicks/quickpicksreluctantyoung.

Young Audiences Arts for Learning NJ & Eastern PA. 2017. "The Cypher Poets—The Secret Cypher Club." YouTube video, January 30, 2:29. https://www.youtube.com/watch?v=hFyBURoUSE4.

Author/Title Index

Content Tag Index

About the Author

LISA KROK, MLIS, MEd, is the adult and teen services manager at Morley Library in the Cleveland, Ohio, area, as well as a former teacher. She is a regular presenter at the Virginia Hamilton Multicultural Literature Conference, and her passion is reaching marginalized teens and reluctant readers through young adult literature. Krok was appointed to the 2019–2020 Presidential Advisory Task Force of the Young Adult Library Services Association (YALSA). In January 2020, she will begin serving on the Best Fiction for Young Adults 2021 committee. Krok was also selected for the 2018 and 2019 Quick Picks for Reluctant Readers teams, which earned her a 2018 YALSA Volunteer of the Year Award. She writes for the *School Library Journal*'s "Teen Librarian Toolbox" and has also blogged for *American Libraries* magazine and YALSA's *The Hub*.